AN
ANTHOLOGY OF
IRISH VERSE

An Anthology of

IRISH VERSE

From Ancient Minstrels'
Songs to Poems
of the Modern Masters

Edited with an Introduction by

PADRAIC COLUM

KILKENNY PRESS
New York

This 1986 edition is published by Kilkenny Press,
distributed by Crown Publishers, Inc., 225 Park
Avenue South, New York, New York 10003, by
arrangement with W. W. Norton and Company, Inc.

Printed and Bound in the United States of America

Library of Congress Cataloging in Publication Data

An Anthology of Irish verse.

Includes indexes.
1. English poetry—Irish authors. 2. Ireland—
Poetry. I. Colum, Padraic, 1881-1972.
PR8851.A58 1986   821'.008'09415
86-27755
ISBN 0-517-62539-3

h g f e d c b a

ACKNOWLEDGMENT

For their generous permission to use poems published in the United States, the editor is indebted to:

Messrs. Brentano, for poems by Francis Ledwidge.

Messrs. Funk and Wagnalls, for poems by Ethna Carbery.

Messrs. Henry Holt, for poems by Francis Carlin.

Mr. W. B. Huebsch, for poems by James Joyce.

The Macmillan Co., for poems by A. E., James Stephens, and W. B. Yeats.

Miss Harriet Munroe, for "On Waking," by Joseph Campbell, "The Apple Tree," by Nancy Campbell, and "The Counsels of O'Riordan the Rann Maker," by T. D. O'Bolger, published in *Poetry,* Chicago.

Messrs. Frederick Stokes, for poems by Thomas Kettle, Thomas MacDonagh, Padraic Pearse and Joseph Plunkett.

For the revised edition of 1948, permissions have been given by the following poets:

Austin Clarke, for "Aisling" (*Collected Poems,* New York, Macmillan Co.).

Denis Devlin, for "Welcome My World" (*Lough Derg, and Other Poems,* New York, Reynal and Hitchcock).

Lyle Donaghy, for "At My Whisper."

Lord Dunsany, for "The Deserted Kingdom" (*Fifty Poems,* New York, Putnam).

Padraic Fallon, for "Mary Hynes."

Robert Farren, for "The Cool Gold Wines of Paradise."

Monk Gibbon, for "From Disciple to Master."

Oliver Gogarty, for "The Forge."

Francis Hackett, for "Sea Dawn."

George Hetherington, for "Charles at the Siege."

Valentin Iremonger, for "While the Summer Trees Were Crying."

Patrick Kavanagh, for "Through the Open Door."

Winifred Letts, for "A Soft Day" (*Songs from Leinster*).

Lord Longford, for "To an Anti-poetical Priest" (*The Dove in the Castle*, Dublin, Hodges Figgis and Co.).

Donagh MacDonagh, for "Dublin Made Me" (*The Hungry Grass*, London, Faber and Faber).

Patrick MacDonogh, for "Be Still As You Are Beautiful."

Francis MacManus, for "Pattern of Saint Brendan."

Brinsley MacNamara, for "On Seeing Swift in Laracor."

Louis MacNeice, for "The Strand."

Thomas McGreevy, for "Aodh Ruadh O'Domhnaill" (*Poems*, London, William Heinemann).

Dermot O'Bryne, for "Dublin Ballad."

Frank O'Connor, for "To Tomaus Costello at the Wars."

Mary Devenport O'Neill, for "The Tramp's Song" (*Prometheus and Other Poems*, London, Jonathan Cape).

Brian O'Nolan (Flann O'Brien), for "Aoibhinn, a leabhráin, do thriall."

Seumas O'Sullivan, for "Sketch."

W. R. Rodgers, for "Life's Circumnavigators."

Blanaid Salkeld, for "No Uneasy Refuge."

Thanks is also rendered to:

Mrs. F. R. Higgins, for permission to use "The Old Jockey" (*Arable Pastures*, New York, Macmillan Co.).

Mrs. Peter Kearney, for permission to use "Down by the Glenside" (*The Bold Fenian Men*, Dublin, Waltons).

Mrs. William Butler Yeats, for permission to use "Under Ben Bulben" (*Last Poems*, New York, Macmillan Co.).

Is buaine port na glór na n-eun
Is buaine focal na toice an t-séaghail.

A leabhráin, gabh amach fá'n saoghal,
Is do gach n-aon dá mbuaileann leat
Aithris cruinn go maireann Gaedhil,
Tréis cleasa claon nan Gall ar fad.

CONTENTS

PART SIX (Our Heritage)

PART SEVEN (Personal Poems)

PART EIGHT (Poems Since 1920)

SLAINTHE!

xiv

AN
ANTHOLOGY OF
IRISH VERSE

INTRODUCTION

I

I should like to call this an Anthology of the Poetry of Ireland rather than an Anthology of Irish Poetry. It is a distinction that has some little difference. It implies, I think, that my effort has been to take the poetry of the people in the mass, and then to make a selection that would be representative of the people rather than representative of individual poets. The usual, and perhaps the better, way to make an anthology is to select poems and group them according to chronological order, or according to an order that has a correspondence in the emotional life of the reader. The first is the method of the Oxford Book of English Verse, and the second is the method of the Golden Treasury of Songs and Lyrics. In this collection,—the last section,—there is an anthology of personal poems that is in chronological order; and there is an anthology of anonymous poems—the second section—that is arranged according to an order that is in the editor's own mind. But the other sections of the anthology are not chronological and are not according to any mental order—they represent a grouping according to dominant national themes.

This method of presentation has been forced upon me by the necessity of arranging the material in the least prosaic way. It would not do, I considered, to arrange the poetry of Ireland according to chronological order. Irish poetry in English is too recent to permit of a number of initial excellencies. Then the racial distinction of Irish poetry in English—in Anglo-Irish poetry—was not an immediate achievement, and so the poetry that would be arranged chronologically would begin without the note of racial distinctiveness. And because so much of Irish poetry comes out of historical situation, because so much of it is based on national themes, the order that has a correspondence in personal emotion, would not be proper to it. The note that I would have it begin on, and the note that I would have recur through the anthology is the note of racial distinctiveness.

II

Ireland is a country that has two literatures—one a literature in Irish—Gaelic literature—that has been cultivated continuously since the eighth century, and the other a literature in English—Anglo-Irish literature—that took its rise in the eighteenth century.

Anglo-Irish literature begins, as an English critic has observed, with Goldsmith and Sheridan humming some urban song as they stroll down an English laneway. That is, it begins chronologically in that way. At the time when Goldsmith and Sheridan might be supposed to be strolling down English laneways, Ireland, for all but a fraction of the people, was a Gaelic-speaking country with a poetry that had many centuries of cultivation. Afterwards English speech began to make its way through the country, and an English-speaking audience became important for Ireland. And then, at the end of the eighteenth century came Thomas Moore, a singer who knew little of the depth or intensity of the Gaelic consciousness, but who, through a fortunate association, was able to get into his songs a racial distinctiveness.

He was born in Dublin, the English-speaking capital, at a time when the Gaelic-speaking South of Ireland had still bards with academic training and tradition—the poets of Munster who were to write the last chapter of the unbroken literary history of Ireland. From the poets with the tradition, from the scholars bred in the native schools, Moore was not able to receive anything. But from those who conserved

5

another part of the national heritage, he was able to receive a great deal.

At the end of the eighteenth century the harpers who had been wandering through the country, playing the beautiful traditional music, were gathered together in Belfast. The music that they were the custodians of was noted down and published by Bunting and by Power. With such collections before them the Irish who had been educated in English ways and English thought were made to realize that they had a national heritage.

Thomas Moore, a born song-writer, began to write English words to this music. Again and again the distinctive rhythms of the music forced a distinctive rhythm upon his verse. Through using the mould of the music, Moore, without being conscious of what he was doing, reproduced again and again the rhythm, and sometimes the structure of Gaelic verse. When Edgar Allen Poe read that lyric of Moore's that begins "At the mid-hour of night," he perceived a distinctive metrical achievement. The poem was written to an ancient Irish air, and its rhythm, like the rhythm of the song that begins "Through grief and through danger," wavering and unemphatic, is distinctively Irish. And Moore not only reproduced the rhythm of Gaelic poetry, but sometimes he reproduced even its metrical structure.

> Silent, O Moyle, be the roar of thy water;
> Break not, ye breezes, your chain of repose,
> While murmuring mournfully, Lir's lonely daughter
> Tells to the night star her tale of woes.

Here is the Gaelic structure with the correspondences all on a single vowel—in this case the vowel "o"—"Moyle," "roar," "repose," "lonely," "woes," with the alliterations "break," "breezes," "tells," "tale," "murmuring," "mournfully." And so, through the association that he made with music, Thomas Moore attained to distinctiveness in certain of his poems.*

* Robert Burns also re-created an Irish form by writing to Irish music in "Their Groves o' Sweet Myrtle." The soldier's song in "The Jolly Beggars" reproduces an Irish form also; the air that Burns wrote this song to may have been an Irish air originally.

6

Back in 1760 MacPherson's "Fragments of Ancient Poetry Collected in the Highlands of Scotland" was published. That medley, unreadable by us to-day, affected the literatures of England, France, Germany and Italy. In the British Islands eager search was made for the Gaelic originals. There were no originals. MacPherson's compositions which he attributed to the Gaelic bard Ossian were, in every sense of the word, original. And yet, as the historian of Scottish Gaelic literature, Dr. Magnus MacLean, has said, the arrival of James MacPherson marked a great moment in the history of all Celtic literatures. "It would seem as if he sounded the trumpet, and the graves of ancient manuscripts were opened, the books were read, and the dead were judged out of the things that were written in them." Those who knew anything of Gaelic literary tradition could not fail to respond to the universal curiosity aroused by the publication of MacPherson's compositions. In Ireland there was a response in the publication of a fragment of the ancient poetry and romance. "The words of this song were suggested by a very ancient Irish story called 'Deirdri, or the lamentable fate of the Sons of Usneach' which has been translated literally from the Gaelic by Mr. O'Flanagan, and upon which it appears that the 'Darthula' of MacPherson is founded," Thomas Moore wrote in a note to the song "Avenging and Bright." Slowly fragments of this ancient literature were revealed and were taken as material for the new Irish poetry.*

After Moore there came another poet who reached a distinctive metrical achievement through his study of the music

* The Ossian of MacPherson (in Ireland Oisin, pronounced Usheen) was supposed to be the poet who had celebrated the lives and actions of the heroic companionship known as the Fianna. The Irish term for this class of poetry is "Fianaidheacht," and an example of it is given in this anthology in "Grainne's sleep-song over Dermuid." At the time when "Ossian" was making appeal to Goethe and Napoleon the great mass of the poetry that was the canon of MacPherson's apochrypha was lying unnoted in the University of Louvain, brought over there by Irish students and scholars. Recently this poetry has been published by the Irish Texts Society (Dunaire Finn, the Poem Book of Finn, edited and translated by Eoin MacNeill).

that Bunting had published. This poet was Samuel Ferguson. He took the trouble to learn Gaelic, and when he translated the words of Irish folk-songs to the music that they were sung to, he created, in half a dozen instances, poems that have a racial distinctiveness. Ferguson had what Moore had not—the ability to convey the Gaelic spirit. Take his "Cashel of Munster":

I'd wed you without herds, without money or rich array,
And I'd wed you on a dewy morn at day-dawn grey;
My bitter word it is, love, that we are not far away
In Cashel town, though the bare deal board were our marriage bed this day.

Here is the wavering rhythm, the unemphatic word-arrangement, that is characteristic of Irish song and some racial character besides. Callanan, too, gets the same effects in his translation of "The Outlaw of Loch Lene":

O many's the day I made good ale in the glen,
That came not from stream nor from malt like the brewing of men;
My bed was the ground, my roof the green wood above,
And all the wealth that I sought, one fair kind glance from my love.

Ferguson's translation of "Cean Dubh Dilis," "Dear Dark Head," makes one of the most beautiful of Irish love songs; it is a poem that carries into English the Gaelic music and the Gaelic feeling; the translation, moreover, is more of a poem than is the original.

Sir Samuel Ferguson was the first Irish poet to attempt a re-telling of any of the ancient sagas. He aimed at doing for "The Tain Bo Cuiligne," the Irish epic cycle, what Tennyson at the time was doing for the Arthurian cycle, presenting it, not as a continuous narrative, but as a series of poetic studies. The figures of the heroic cycle, however, were too primitive, too elemental, too full of their own sort of humour for Ferguson to take them on their own terms. He made

8

them conform a good deal to Victorian rectitudes. And yet, it has to be said that he blazed a trail in the trackless region of Celtic romance; the prelude to his studies, "The Tain Quest," written in a heady ballad metre, is quite a stirring poem, and his "Conairy" manages to convey a sense of vast and mysterious action. It was to Ferguson that W. B. Yeats turned when he began his deliberate task of creating a national literature for Ireland.

With Sir Samuel Ferguson there is associated a poet whom he long outlived, James Clarence Mangan. Mangan was a great rhapsodist if not a great poet. He was an original metrical artist, and it is possible that Edgar Allen Poe learnt some metrical devices from him.* The themes that this poet seized on were not from Irish romance, but were from the history of the Irish overthrow. And what moved him to his greatest expression were the themes that has a terrible desolation or an unbounded exultation—Brian's palace overthrown and his dynasty cut oft; the Princes of the line of Conn dying unnoted in exile; the heroic chief of the Clann Maguire fleeing unfriended through the storm; or else it is Dark Rosaleen with her "holy, delicate white hands" to whom all is offered in a rapture of dedication. Mangan incarnated in Anglo-Irish poetry the bardic spirit of the seventeenth and eighteenth centuries, and the sigh that Egan O'Rahilly breathed, "A mo Thir, A mo Gradh," "O my Land, O my Love," is breathed through all his memorable poetry. He had the privilege of creating the most lovely of all feminine representations of Ireland, and in "Dark Rosaleen" he has made the greatest, because the most spiritual, patriotic poem in the world's literature. One has to describe the best of Mangan's poems as translations, but in doing so, one is conscious that one has to extend unduly the meaning of the word. And yet, the impulse and the theme has come to him through the work of another, and this not only in the case of poetry he took from Irish sources, but in the poetry that he drew from German and Arabic sources.

Mangan's poems were published in the forties. There was

* Mangan published in the Dublin University Magazine, a publication which Poe had opportunities of seeing. Compare with Poe's Mangan's use of repetitions and internal rhymes.

then a conscious literary movement in Ireland. It went with the European democratic movement, with the coming to consciousness of many European nationalities. At the time the Finns were collecting their Magic Songs that were to be woven into the enchanting epic of the Kalavala, and the Bohemians were making their first efforts to revive their distinctive culture. And the Irish, with their ancient literary cultivation and their varied literary production, might be thought to be in a position to create a literature at once national and modern, intellectual and heroic. Under the leadership of Thomas Davis a movement of criticism and scholarship was inaugurated—a movement that might be looked to to have fruit in a generation.

Then came the terrible disaster of the famine—of the double famine, for the famine of '47 followed the famine of '46. The effect of this national disaster (until the war no European people had suffered such a calamity in two hundred years) was the making of a great rent in the social life. How it affected everything that belonged to the imagination may be guessed at from a sentence written by George Petrie. He made the great collection of Irish music, but in the preface to his collection he laments that he entered the field too late. What impressed him most about the Ireland after the famine was, as he says, "the sudden silence of the fields." Before, no one could have walked a roadway without hearing music and song; now there was cessation, and this meant a break in the whole tradition.

And what Petrie noted with regard to music was true for song and saga. The song perished with the tune. The older generation who were the custodians of the national tradition were the first to go down to the famine graves. And in the years that followed the people had little heart for the remembering of "old, unhappy, far-off things and battles long ago." The history of Ireland since is a record of recovery and relapse after an attack that almost meant the death of the race.

III

In 1889, ending the account of Gaelic literature that he gave in his Literary History of Ireland, Dr. Douglas Hyde wrote, "The question whether the national language is to become wholly extinct like the Cornish is one which must be decided in the next ten years." A half a century and more has gone by and the question has not been decided. But it would have been decided; Irish to-day would have been virtually extinct if Douglas Hyde, poet, scholar, folk-lorist and great leader, had not put himself at the head of a popular movement, the Gaelic League, for the restoration of Irish as a vernacular and a literary medium. The new Irish state pegged down the gains made by the movement and put Irish in all the schools. To-day poems, essays and dramas written in Irish have a fair public. And in half the Irish poets now writing in English Gaelic influences on theme, rhythm and idiom are strongly marked.

But in pegging down the gains made by the popular movement, the national state acted with a certain intolerance, with an attitude that discounted the Anglo-Irish contribution to Irish culture. The result has been, in certain quarters, a coolness and even an antipathy to the Gaelicising effort. In Eire to-day everyone of the younger generation can read works in Irish or can hear long and elaborate poems of eighteenth century Gaelic poets over the radio. Irish poets writing in English, consequently, are aware of another approach to poetry, have access to another material, know another idiom. Many have availed themselves of these factors and have brought freshness and richness into their poetry. And even the poets who have not done so, by reacting against Gaelicism have had to sharpen a different conviction and find a different style. There are poets who go back to O'Rahilly and Raftery and express themselves in a Gaelic mode; there are poets who, aware of this mode, turn from it in order to be less local or more modern: their contact with Gaelicism has made their work unlike what it would have been if the influences were

11

from English poetry solely. For quite some time, I believe, Irish poetry in either mode will show cross-fertilization.

Poetry written in English in Ireland has had a broken history. The use of Middle English in Ireland began in the thirteenth and ended at the beginning of the seventeenth century. But out of what was written in this long period surprisingly little remains to us. English which had for competitors not only Irish, but Norman-French and Latin, spread in the thirteenth, but in the centuries following declined almost to extinction. The Norman Statute of Kilkenny forbade the use of Irish in the Pale, that is in the eastern counties that had an English-speaking population. The year after this Statute was enacted the Fourth Earl of Desmond was appointed Justiciar for Ireland. This Earl (Gerald the Rhymer) wrote poetry in Irish that still survives; he was, in fact, the originator in Irish of the poetry of courtly love. And so we have an instance of a great official and an aristocrat whose other language was Norman-French turning, not to English (the burgher language), but to Irish, for the language and form of aristocratic poetry.

Modern English came to Ireland in the seventeenth century, and gradually spread over the whole country. This new English culture was moulded to some extent by the older English culture in Ireland. The link between the two is Richard Stanihurst. Stanihurst was a Catholic and belonged to the Anglo-Ireland that was more Norman than Saxon. The succeeding writers were Protestant and of the new times. But their intellectual chieftains, Swift and Berkeley, went to the school that Stanihurst was educated in, a famous school in Kilkenny that had been founded by the Norman and, until then, Catholic house of Ormond. With Swift and Berkeley, Goldsmith came under that influence. And this leads to the claim that in Anglo-Irish literature, even when it is uninfluenced by Gaelic, there is a distinctive element. "The Irish, born and educated in Ireland, were always in the preponderance among educated men in Ireland, and there was a true continuance of tradition; which means that the true roots of culture in Ireland at present (except for the real Gaelic elements in the west) are to be found in the Norman period, A.D. 1200-1500, thus making Ireland quite parallel to England and Scotland in each of which a fusion of Norman with local elements of population took place in the same period."

Modern English did not emerge victorious from the struggle with Irish until the middle of the nineteenth century, and its victory then was largely due to the defeatism produced in the

Irish people by the famine of 1846-47. This new English in producing Swift produced the modern Anglo-Irish literature. A century before Swift's time, when the older English culture in Ireland was falling to pieces and the Gaelic culture was being penalized, one who was a priest and a scholar wrote a book which though not intrinsically great had, because of its fervour and irreplaceable knowledge, an historical effect. The writer's name shows he was of Norman-Irish descent; it was Geoffrey Keating; his book was "Foras Feasa ar Eirinn."

"Keating's great work," writes Dr. Myles Dillon, "written in the early seventeenth century, in smooth and graceful prose, was a triumph over defeat, and shows that the Irish language was never stronger nor finer than when the last hope was shattered at Kinsale." It was by way of being history. But into the historical scheme, Keating, like other scholars prior to the time of histoiical criticism, fitted the divine beings of mythology and the personages of the sagas. His book helped to keep a national consciousness amongst Irish people who spoke and read Gaelic through the terrible period of their downfall and dispersal. It began to be circulated—it was not published in the modern sense of the word—in the middle of the seventeenth century.

Parts of it read like the work of a modern refugee who has put his soul into a protest against enemy destructiveness and enemy propaganda, and into making a statement of his own that will be acceptable to right-thinking men. But it was the non-historical elements in "Foras Feasa ar Eirinn" that was to give it its appeal for later generations—the fragments of sagas about Finn and the Red Branch. Through this work in translation English-speaking Irish people of the eighteenth and nineteenth centuries got to know something of "the matter of Ireland."

A few amateurs of the eighteenth century attempted histories of Ireland taking their material from Keating. Their work was mediocre. Then in the 1880's a student named Standish James O'Grady read one of these quasi-historical works and got an inspiration from it. Standish James O'Grady had an historical feeling and an epic kind of imagination; he divined a bardic element behind the prosaic relation; meditating on the figures of Conn, Eoghan, Cuchullain, Finn, he saw they were larger than life and somehow charged with destiny: they did not belong to a finished record but to a future that still has to be fulfilled. Out of this idea he wrote his "Bardic History of Ireland." He had other material than Keating to draw on; by this time the work of really great scholars, O'Curry and O'Donovan, had added new domains to Irish tradition. The new writers who attempted to deal with the saga and epic material drew inspiration from O'Grady's Bardic History.

Here then are two traditions that will continue to form Irish poetry. And beside them is the tradition of folk poetry and popular balladry. But Irish poetry, it seems to me, is breaking away from many traditional influences. The younger poets seem to have acquired an individuality that is sometimes harsh. I do not say that, leaving out certain names, they are gainers or losers by this: it could be maintained that they have lost a quality that was to the good, the freshness, say, that one finds in some of the younger contemporaries of Yeats. There is less of the countryside in them, less of something hereditary, and more of an individual outlook. As one reads some of these recent poems one may recall such a poem as Yeats' "Song of the Old Mother": she rises at dawn and blows the seed of the fire into a glow; she goes on with the household tasks while the young take it easy because they have their dreams; she works until the fire has to be covered again, "for the seed of the fire gets feeble and cold." One feels that the old mother is aware that all she does has been done for generations, and that there is something over and above hardship in her doing of them—felt custom and felt community are in what she does. In what she says there is little assertiveness; it goes with the traditional lilt in the verse. But the awareness of custom and community is fading out of the Irish countryside; the poets of to-day seem to have little support in the pieties that meant so much in the days of W. B. Yeats and Douglas Hyde. The older poets, when they dealt with the countryside, took their matter from the folk; the present-day poets take theirs from the individual peasant.

Still, there is something of community in Irish poetry of to-day. And one can find a quality, I think, that is unusual in modern poetry—a quality that is entertaining. Sometimes that entertaining quality comes from the speech rhythms of the verse, from words that are colloquial and at the same time unusual, a statement now and again that is witty or humourous. These are surfaces and there is something deeper. Ultimately the entertainment that is in present-day Irish poetry comes from the poets' attitude to poetry: for them, or for most of them, poetry is not a private meditation but comes out of a topic that has a group interest, and it comes, one can think, as a flourish to a heady conversation.

14

IV

In the second section of this Anthology there is a collection of songs mainly anonymous—the songs of the street and the countryside. These songs are a distinctive national possession, and, in many cases, they have been a medium through which Gaelic influences have passed into English.

Certain traditional songs of the countryside have been passing over from Gaelic into English ever since English began to be used familiarly here and there in the countryside. Not so many, however; very few of the famous Gaelic songs have been changed from Gaelic into English by the country people themselves. But as English became a little more familiar, or Gaelic a little less familiar, translations were made, or rather, transferences took place with the music remaining to keep the mould. Thus a technique that was more Gaelic than English grew up in the country places; and even before scholarship made any revelation of Gaelic literature to the cultivated, an interpenetration of the two literatures was taking place.

These anonymous songs are of two distinct types—the song that has in it some personal emotion or imagining; that comes out of a reverie.

My love is like the sun,
That in the firmament does run,
And always is constant and true;
But his is like the moon,
That wanders up and down,
And every month it is new.

15

and the song that has in it the sentiment of the crowd:

> The French are on the say,
> Says the Shan Van Vocht,
> The French are on the say,
> They'll be here without delay,
> And the Orange will decay,
> Says the Shan Van Vocht.

The first is the song of the countryside as it is found all the world over, the second is that very characteristic Irish product, the street-song or ballad.

It is the business of the singer of the street-song and of the man who makes the verses for him to hold the casual crowd that happens to be at the fair or the market. The maker of the street-song cannot prepare the mind of his audience for his story, and so he has to deal with an event the significance of which has been already felt—a political happening, a murder, an execution. The maker of the street-song has to make himself the chorus in the drama of daily happenings. He has always to be dramatic:

> I met with Napper Tandy, and he took me by the hand,
> And he said, "How is poor Ireland, and how does she stand?"

Or:

> O then tell me, Shaun O'Farrell, why do you hurry so?

More than any other Anglo-Irish verse product, these street-songs show the influences of Gaelic music and the technique of Gaelic poetry. One finds stanzas the rhythm of which reproduces the distinctive rhythm of the music:

> On the blood-crimsoned plains the Irish Brigade nobly stood,
> They fought at Orleans till the streams they ran with their blood;
> Far away from their land, in the arms of death they repose,

16

For they fought for poor France, and they fell by the hands
of her foes.

A stanza of Moore's has been already quoted to show a
Gaelic verse-structure, with all the correspondences based on
a single vowel. In the street-songs, and the more personal
songs of the country-side, made as they have been, by men
more familiar with the Gaelic than with the English way of
making verse, one often finds the same elaborate and distinctive structure. Take, for instance, the song in the second
section called "The Boys of Mullaghbaun," in which all the
correspondences are on the broad "a":

On a Monday morning *early,* as my wandering steps did
lade me,
Down by a farmer's *station,* and the meadows and free lands,
I heard great *lamentation* the small birds they were *making,*
Saying, "We'll have no more *engagements* with the Boys of
Mullaghbaun!"

Thus music and the memory of Gaelic verse has left in the
Irish country places a technique that is as much Gaelic as
English. In not all of them, however; in parts of Ulster,
Scots song has had influence and currency.

V

One of the characteristics of Irish poetry according to Thomas MacDonagh is a certain naiveté. "An Irish poet," he says, "if he be individual, if he be original, if he be national, speaks, almost stammers, in one of the two fresh languages of this country; in Irish (modern Irish, newly schooled by Europe), or in Anglo-Irish, English as we speak it in Ireland. . . . Such an Irish poet can still express himself in the simplest terms of life and of the common furniture of life." *

Thomas MacDonagh is speaking here of the poetry that is being written to-day, of the poetry that comes out of a community that is still mainly agricultural, that is still close to the soil, that has but few possessions. And yet, with this naiveté there must go a great deal of subtility. "Like the Japanese," says Kuno Meyer, "the Celts were always quick to take an artistic hint; they avoid the obvious and the commonplace; the half-said thing to them is dearest." † This is said of the poetry written in Ireland many centuries ago, but the subtility that the critic credits the Celts with is still a racial heritage.

Irish poetry begins with a dedication—a dedication of the race to the land. The myth of the invasion tells that the first act of the invaders was the invoking of the land of Ireland—its hills, its rivers, its forests, its cataracts. Amergin, the

* Literature in Ireland.
† Ancient Irish Poetry.

18

first poet, pronounced the invocation from one of their ships, thereby dedicating the Milesian race to the mysterious land. That dedication is in many poems made since Amergin's time —the dedication of the poet to the land, of the race to the land.

When the Milesian Celts drew in their ships they found, peopling the island, not a folk to be destroyed or mingled with, but a remote and ever-living race, the Tuatha De Danaan, the Golden Race of Hesiod. Between the Milesians and the Tuatha De Danaan a truce was made with a partitioning of the country. To the Milesians went the upper surface and the accessible places, and to the De Danaans went the subterranean and the inaccessible places of the land. Thus, in Ireland, the Golden Race did not go down before the men of the Iron Race. They stayed to give glimpses of more lovely countries, more beautiful lovers, more passionate and adventurous lives to princes and peasants for more than a thousand years. And so an enchantment has stayed in this furthest of European lands—an enchantment that still lives through the Fairy Faith of the people, and that left in the old literature an allurement that, through the Lays of Marie de France, through the memorable incidents in the Tristan and Iseult story, through the quests which culminated outside of Ireland in the marvellous legend of the Grail, has passed into European literature.

Whether it has or has not to do with the prosaic issue of self-determination, it is certain that Irish poetry in these latter days is becoming more, and not less national. But it is no longer national in the deliberate way that Thomas Davis thought it should be national, as "condensed and gem-like history," * or, as his example in ballad-making tended to make it national, by an insistence upon collective political feeling.

> Strongbow's force, and Henry's wile,
> Tudor's wrath and Stuart's guile,

* "National poetry . . . binds us to the land by its condensed and gem-like history. It . . . fires us in action, prompts our invention, sheds a grace beyond the power of luxury round our homes, it is the recognized envoy of our minds among all mankind, and to all time."

And iron Strafford's tiger jaws,
And brutal Brunswick's penal laws;
Not forgetting Saxon faith,
Not forgetting Norman scath,
Not forgetting William's word,
Not forgetting Cromwell's sword.

No, Irish poetry is no longer national in the deliberate or the claimant way. But it is becoming national as the Irish landscape is national, as the tone and gesture of the Irish peasant is national.

PART I
THE HOUSE, THE ROAD, THE FIELD, THE FAIR, AND THE FIRESIDE

A Poem To Be Said on Hearing the Birds Sing

A FRAGRANT prayer upon the air
My child taught me,
Awaken there, the morn is fair,
The birds sing free;
Now dawns the day, awake and pray,
And bend the knee;
The Lamb who lay beneath the clay
Was slain for thee.

Translated by DR. DOUGLAS HYDE.

The Song of the Old Mother

I RISE in the dawn, and I kneel and blow
Till the seed of the fire flicker and glow;
And then I must scrub and bake and sweep
Till stars are beginning to blink and peep;
And the young lie long and dream in their bed
Of the matching of ribbons for bosom and head,
And their day goes over in idleness,
And they sigh if the wind but lift a tress:
While I must work because I am old,
And the seed of the fire gets feeble and cold.

WILLIAM BUTLER YEATS.

On Waking

SLEEP, gray brother of death,
  Has touched me,
And passed on.

I arise, facing the east—
Pearl-doored sanctuary
From which the light,
Hand-linked with dew and fire,
Dances.

Hail, essence, hail!
Fill the windows of my soul
With beauty:
Pierce and renew my bones:
Pour knowledge into my heart
As wine.

Cualann is bright before thee.
Its rocks melt and swim:
The secret they have kept
From the ancient nights of darkness
Flies like a bird.

What mourns?
Cualann's secret flying.
A lost voice
In endless fields.
What rejoices?
My voice lifted praising thee.

Praise! Praise! Praise!
Praise out of the trumpets, whose brass
Is the unyoked strength of bulls;

Praise upon the harp, whose strings
Are the light movement of birds;
Praise of leaf, praise of blossom,
Praise of the red-fibred clay;
Praise of grass,
Fire-woven veil of the temple;
Praise of the shapes of clouds;
Praise of the shadows of wells;
Praise of worms, of fetal things,
And of things in time's thought
Not yet begotten.
To thee, queller of sleep,
Looser of the snare of death.

JOSEPH CAMPBELL.

A Day in Ireland

FOUR sharp scythes sweeping—in concert keeping
　　The rich-robed meadow's broad bosom o'er,
Four strong men mowing, with bright health glowing
　　A long green swath spread each man before;
With sinews springing—my keen blade swinging,—
　　I strode—the fourth man in that blithe band;
As stalk of corn that summer morn,
　　The scythe felt light in my stalwart hand.

Oh, King of Glory!　How changed my story,
　　Since in youth's noontide—long, long ago,
I mowed that meadow—no cloudy shadow
　　Between my brow and the hot sun's glow;
Fair girls raking the hay—and making
　　The fields resound with their laugh and glee,
Their voices ringing—than cuckoo's singing,
　　Made music sweeter by far to me.

Bees hovered over the honied clover,
　　Then nestward hied upon wings of light;
No use in trying to trace them flying—
　　One brief low hum and they're out of sight,
On downy thistle bright insects nestle,
　　Or flutter skyward on painted wings,
At times alighting on flowers inviting—
　　'Twas pleasant watching the airy things.

From hazel bushes came songs of thrushes
  And blackbirds—sweeter than harper's lay;
While high in ether—with sun-tipped feather—
  The skylark warbled his anthem gay;
With throats distended, sweet linnets blended
  A thousand notes in one glorious chime,
Oh, King Eternal, 'twas life supernal
  In beauteous Erin, that pleasant time.
                    Translated by MICHAEL CAVANAGH.

A Drover

TO MEATH of the pastures,
   From wet hills by the sea,
Through Leitrim and Longford
Go my cattle and me.

I hear in the darkness
Their slipping and breathing.
I name them the bye-ways
They're to pass without heeding.

Then the wet, winding roads,
Brown bogs with black water;
And my thoughts on white ships
And the King o' Spain's daughter.

O! farmer, strong farmer!
You can spend at the fair
But your face you must turn
To your crops and your care.

And soldiers—red soldiers!
You've seen many lands;
But you walk two by two,
And by captain's commands.

O! the smell of the beasts,
The wet wind in the morn;
And the proud and hard earth
Never broken for corn;

And the crowds at the fair,
The herds loosened and blind,
Loud words and dark faces
And the wild blood behind.

(O! strong men with your best
I would strive breast to breast
I could quiet your herds
With my words, with my words.)

I will bring you, my kine,
Where there's grass to the knee;
But you'll think of scant croppings
Harsh with salt of the sea.

PADRAIC COLUM.

The Blind Man at the Fair

O TO be blind!
　　To know the darkness that I know.
The stir I hear is empty wind,
The people idly come and go.

The sun is black, tho' warm and kind,
The horsemen ride, the streamers blow
Vainly in the fluky wind,
For all is darkness where I go.

The cattle bellow to their kind,
The mummers dance, the jugglers throw,
The thimble-rigger speaks his mind—
But all is darkness where I go.

I feel the touch of womankind,
Their dresses flow as white as snow;
But beauty is a withered rind
For all is darkness where I go.

Last night the moon of Lammas shined,
Rising high and setting low;
But light is nothing to the blind—
All, all is darkness where they go.

White roads I walk with vacant mind,
White cloud-shapes round me drifting slow,
White lilies waving in the wind—
And darkness everywhere I go.

　　　　　　　　　JOSEPH CAMPBELL.

Market Women's Cries

COME buy my fine wares,
  Plums, apples and pears.
A hundred a penny,
In conscience too many:
Come, will you have any?
My children are seven,
I wish them in Heaven;
My husband 's a sot,
With his pipe and his pot,
  Not a farthen will gain them,
And I must maintain them.

ONIONS

Come, follow me by the smell,
Here are delicate onions to sell;
I promise to use you well.
They make the blood warmer,
You'll feed like a farmer;
For this is every cook's opinion,
No savoury dish without an onion;
But, lest your kissing should be spoiled,
Your onions must be thoroughly boiled:

Or else you may spare
Your mistress a share,
The secret will never be known:
She cannot discover
The breath of her lover,
But think it as sweet as her own.

HERRINGS

Be not sparing,
Leave off swearing.
Buy my herring
Fresh from Malahide,
Better never was tried.
Come, eat them with pure fresh butter and mustard,
Their bellies are soft, and as white as a custard.
Come, sixpence a dozen, to get me some bread,
Or, like my own herrings, I soon shall be dead.

JONATHAN SWIFT.

John-John

I DREAMT last night of you, John-John,
  And thought you called to me;
And when I woke this morning, John,
Yourself I hoped to see;
But I was all alone, John-John,
Though still I heard your call;
I put my boots and bonnet on,
And took my Sunday shawl,
And went full sure to find you, John,
    At Nenagh fair.

The fair was just the same as then,
Five years ago to-day,
When first you left the thimble-men
And came with me away;
For there again were thimble-men
And shooting galleries,
And card-trick men and maggie-men,
Of all sorts and degrees;
But not a sight of you, John-John,
    Was anywhere.

I turned my face to home again,
And called myself a fool
To think you'd leave the thimble-men
And live again by rule,
To go to mass and keep the fast
And till the little patch;

My wish to have you home was past
Before I raised the latch
And pushed the door and saw you, John,
    Sitting down there.

How cool you came in here, begad,
As if you owned the place!
But rest yourself there now, my lad,
'Tis good to see your face;
My dream is out, and now by it
I think I know my mind:
At six o'clock this house you'll quit,
And leave no grief behind;—
But until six o'clock, John-John,
    My bit you'll share.

The neighbours' shame of me began
When first I brought you in;
To wed and keep a tinker man
They thought a kind of sin;
But now this three years since you've gone
'Tis pity me they do,
And that I'd rather have, John-John,
Than that they'd pity you,
Pity for me and you, John-John,
    I could not bear.

Oh, you're my husband right enough,
But what's the good of that?
You know you never were the stuff
To be the cottage cat,
To watch the fire and hear me lock
The door and put out Shep—
But there, now, it is six o'clock
And time for you to step.
God bless and keep you far, John-John!
    And that's my prayer.
          THOMAS MACDONAGH.

No Miracle

THEY had a tale on which to gloat,
The gossips sitting in a row:
How Feylimeed took wife by throat
And broke her beauty with a blow.

And one, and then another, said:
Ah, fortunate if now she die;
For piteous is a cloth-bound head
Instead of beauty's flashing eye.

Else to some desert let her go
From women's words and eyes of men,
But ancient Eefa whispered low:
"Simply you read the story then."

No other word old Eefa spoke
But smiling blinked from side to side,
Till Enna, breathless, on them broke
Her mouth and eyes with horror wide.

"He gropes his way, his eyes are out!"
"Who gropes his way?" "Why, Faylimeed!"
"The blind cat's fingers, without doubt
Got at them sleeping?" "Nay, indeed,

"No fingers but his own plucked, flung
Them dazzling in the sullen tide,
For ah, they say his heart was wrung
To see the wreck of beauty's pride."

35

Then Eefa whispered from her place:
"As Faylimeed gripped wife by throat
Her eyes flashed love into his face
And his heart blazed while his hand smote."
DANIEL CORKERY.

Let Us Be Merry Before We Go

IF SADLY thinking, with spirits sinking,
  Could, more than drinking, my cares compose
A cure for sorrow from sighs I'd borrow,
And hope to-morrow would end my woes.
But as in wailing there's nought availing,
And Death unfailing will strike the blow,
Then for that reason, and for a season,
Let us be merry before we go.

To joy a stranger, a wayworn ranger,
In every danger my course I've run;
Now hope all ending, and death befriending,
His last aid lending, my cares are done.
No more a rover, or hapless lover,
My griefs are over—my glass runs low;
Then for that reason, and for a season,
Let us be merry before we go.

JOHN PHILPOT CURRAN.

Had I a Golden Pound

HAD I a golden pound to spend,
   My love should mend and sew no more.
And I would buy her a little quern,
Easy to turn on the kitchen floor.

And for her windows curtains white,
With birds in flight and flowers in bloom,
To face with pride the road to town,
And mellow down her sunlit room.

And with the silver change we'd prove
The Truth of Love to life's own end,
With hearts the years could but embolden,
Had I a golden pound to spend.

FRANCIS LEDWIDGE.

The Coolun

AH, HAD you seen the Coolun,
   Walking down by the cuckoo's street,
With the dew of the meadow shining
On her milk-white twinkling feet.
My love she is, and my colleen óg
And she dwells in Bal'nagar;
And she bears the palm of beauty bright
From the fairest that in Erin are.

In Bal'nagar is the Coolun:
Like the berry on the bough her cheek;
Bright beauty dwells forever
On her fair neck and ringlets sleek;
Oh, sweeter is her mouth's soft music
Than the lark or thrush at dawn,
Or the blackbird in the greenwood singing
Farewell to the setting sun.

Rise up, my boy! make ready
My horse, for I forth would ride,
To follow the modest damsel,
Where she walks on the green hill-side:
For ever since youth were we plighted,
In faith, troth, and wedlock true—
Oh, she's sweeter to me nine times over
Than organ or cuckoo!

For ever since my childhood
I loved the fair and darling child;
But our people came between us,
And with lucre our pure love defiled:
Oh, my woe it is, and my bitter pain,
And I weep it night and day,
That the colleen bán of my early love
Is torn from my heart away.

Sweetheart and faithful treasure,
Be constant still, and true;
Nor for want of herds and houses
Leave one who would ne'er leave you.
I'll pledge you the blessed Bible,
Without and eke within,
That the faithful God will provide for us,
Without thanks to kith or kin.

Oh, love, do you remember
When we lay all night alone,
Beneath the ash in the winter storm,
When the oak wood round did groan?
No shelter then from the storm had we,
The bitter blast or sleet,
But your gown to wrap about our heads,
And my coat round our feet.

Translated by SIR SAMUEL FERGUSON.

Have You Been at Carrick?

HAVE you been at Carrick, and saw my true-love there?
     And saw you her features, all beautiful, bright, and fair?
Saw you the most fragrant, flowering, sweet apple-tree?—
Oh! saw you my loved one, and pines she in grief like me?

I have been at Carrick, and saw thy own true-love there;
And saw, too, her features, all beautiful, bright and fair;
And saw the most fragrant, flowering, sweet apple-tree—
I saw thy loved one—she pines not in grief, like thee!

Five guineas would price every tress of her golden hair—
Then think what a treasure her pillow at night to share,
These tresses thick-clustering and curling around her brow—
Oh, Ringlet of Fairness! I'll drink to thy beauty now! !

When seeking to slumber, my bosom is rent with sighs—
I toss on my pillow till morning's blest beams arise;
No aid, bright Beloved! can reach me save God above,
For a blood-lake is formed of the light of my eyes with love!

Until yellow Autumn shall usher the Paschal day,
And Patrick's gay festival come in its train alway—
Although through my coffin the blossoming boughs shall grow,
My love on another I'll never in life bestow!

Lo! yonder the maiden illustrious, queen-like, high,
With long-flowing tresses adown to her sandal-tie—
Swan, fair as the lily, descended of high degree,
A myriad of welcomes, dear maid of my heart, to thee!

Translated by EDWARD WALSH

The Stars Stand Up in the Air

THE stars stand up in the air,
　The sun and the moon are gone,
The strand of its waters is bare.
And her sway is swept from the swan.

The cuckoo was calling all day,
Hid in the branches above,
How my stóirín is fled away,
'Tis my grief that I gave her my love.

Three things through love I see—
Sorrow and sin and death—
And my mind reminding me
That this doom I breathe with my breath.

But sweeter than violin or lute
Is my love—and she left me behind.
I wish that all music were mute,
And I to all beauty were blind.

She's more shapely than swan by the strand,
She's more radiant than grass after dew,
She's more fair than the stars where they stand—
'Tis my grief that her ever I knew!
　　Translated by THOMAS MACDONAGH.

Dear Dark Head

PUT your head, darling, darling, darling,
  Your darling black head my heart above;
Oh, mouth of honey, with the thyme for fragrance,
  Who with heart in breast could deny you love?

Oh, many and many a young girl for me is pining,
  Letting her locks of gold to the cold wind free,
For me, the foremost of our gay young fellows;
  But I'd leave a hundred, pure love, for thee!

Then put your head, darling, darling, darling,
  Your darling black head my heart above;
Oh, mouth of honey, with the thyme for fragrance,
  Who, with heart in breast, could deny you love?
    Translated by SIR SAMUEL FERGUSON.

Pearl of the White Breast

THERE'S a colleen fair as May,
  For a year and for a day,
 I've sought by every way her heart to gain
There's no art of tongue or eye
Fond youths with maidens try,
  But I've tried with ceaseless sigh, yet tried in vain.

If to France or far-off Spain
She'd cross the watery main,
  To see her face again the sea I'd brave.
And if 'tis Heaven's decree
That mine she may not be,
  May the Son of Mary me in mercy save!

O thou blooming milk-white dove,
To whom I've given true love,
  Do not ever thus reprove my constancy.
There are maidens would be mine,
With wealth in hand and kine,
  If my heart would but incline to turn from thee.

But a kiss with welcome bland
And a touch of thy dear hand
  Are all that I demand, wouldst thou not spurn;
For if not mine, dear girl,
O Snowy-Breasted Pearl!
  May I never from the fair with life return!
                    Translated by GEORGE PETRIE.

Country Sayings

THE closing of an Autumn evening is like the running of a
hound across the moor.

Night is a good herd: she brings all creatures home.

Lie down with the lamb
And rise with the bird,
From the time you see a harrow and a man behind it
Until you see stacks of turf and cocks of hay.

Cois na Teineadh

WHERE glows the Irish hearth with peat
　　There lives a subtle spell—
The faint blue smoke, the gentle heat,
The moorland odours tell.

Of white roads winding by the edge
Of bare, untamèd land,
Where dry stone wall or ragged hedge
Runs wide on either hand.

To cottage lights that lure you in
From rainy Western skies;
And by the friendly glow within
Of simple talk, and wise,

And tales of magic, love or arms
From days when princes met
To listen to the lay that charms
The Connacht peasant yet,

There Honour shines through passions dire,
There beauty blends with mirth—
Wild hearts, ye never did aspire
Wholly for things of earth!

Cold, cold this thousand years—yet still
On many a time-stained page
Your pride, your truth, your dauntless will,
Burn on from age to age.

And still around the fires of peat
Live on the ancient days;
There still do living lips repeat
The old and deathless lays.

And when the wavering wreaths ascend
Blue in the evening air,
The soul of Ireland seems to bend
Above her children there.

T. W. ROLLESTON.

The Ballad of Father Gilligan

THE old priest, Peter Gilligan,
　Was weary night and day;
For half his flock were in their beds,
Or under green sods lay.

Once, while he nodded on a chair,
At the moth-hour of eve,
Another poor man sent for him,
And he began to grieve.

"I have no rest, nor joy, nor peace,
For people die and die";
And after cried he, "God forgive!
My body spake, not I!"

He knelt, and leaning on the chair
He prayed and fell asleep,
And the moth-hour went from the fields,
And stars began to peep.

They slowly into millions grew,
And leaves shook in the wind,
And God covered the world with shade,
And whispered to mankind.

Upon the time of sparrow chirp
When the moths come once more,
The old priest, Peter Gilligan,
Stood upright on the floor.

"Mavrone, mavrone! the man has died,
While I slept on the chair."
He roused his horse out of its sleep,
And rode with little care.

He rode now as he never rode,
By rocky lane and fen;
The sick man's wife opened the door:
"Father! you come again."

"And is the poor man dead?" he cried.
"He died an hour ago."
The old priest, Peter Gilligan,
In grief swayed to and fro.

"When you were gone, he turned and died
As merry as a bird."
The old priest, Peter Gilligan,
He knelt him at that word.

"He who hath made the night of stars
For souls who tire and bleed,
Sent one of His great angels down
To help me in my need.

"He who is wrapped in purple robes,
With planets in His care,
Had pity on the least of things
Asleep upon a chair."
                    WILLIAM BUTLER YEATS.

Ballad of Douglas Bridge

ON Douglas Bridge I met a man
  Who lived adjacent to Strabane,
    Before the English hung him high
For riding with O'Hanlon.

The eyes of him were just as fresh
As when they burned within the flesh;
    And his boot-legs were wide apart
From riding with O'Hanlon.

"God save you, Sir," I said with fear,
"You seem to be a stranger here."
    "Not I," said he, "nor any man
Who rides with Count O'Hanlon.

"I know each glen from North Tyrone
To Monaghan, and I've been known
    By every clan and parish, since
I rode with Count O'Hanlon."

"Before that time," said he to me,
"My fathers owned the land you see;
    But they are now among the moors
A-riding with O'Hanlon."

"Before that time," said he with pride,
"My fathers rode where now they ride
    As Rapparees, before the time
Of trouble and O'Hanlon."

"Good night to you, and God be with
The tellers of the tale and myth,
　　For they are of the spirit-stuff
That rides with Count O'Hanlon."

"Good night to you," said I, "and God
Be with the chargers, fairy-shod,
　　That bear the Ulster heroes forth
To ride with Count O'Hanlon."

On Douglas Bridge we parted, but
The Gap o' Dreams is never shut,
　　To one whose saddled soul to-night
Rides out with Count O'Hanlon.
Francis Carlin.

Homecoming

JOLLY PHOEBUS his car to the coach-house had driven,
  And unharnessed his high-mettled horses of light;
He gave them a feed from the manger of heaven,
  And rubbed them and littered them up for the night.

Then down to the kitchen he leisurely strode,
  Where Thetis, the housemaid, was sipping her tea;
He swore he was tired with that damn'd up-hill road,
  He'd have none of her slops nor hot water, not he.

So she took from the corner a little cruiskeen.
  Well filled with nectar Apollo loves best;
(From the neat Bog of Allen, some pretty poteen),
  And he tippled his quantum and staggered to rest.

His many-caped box-coat around him he thréw,
  For his bed, faith, 'twas dampish, and none of the best;
All above him the clouds their bright fringed curtains drew,
  And the tuft of his nightcap lay red in the west.
                                        ANONYMOUS.

52

When Kian O'Hara's Cup Was Passed to Turlough O'Carolan

WERE I west in green Arran,
　　Or south in Glanmore,
Where the long ships come laden
　　With claret in store;
Yet I'd rather than shiploads
　　Of claret, and ships,
Have your white cup, O'Hara,
　　Up full to my lips.

But why seek in numbers
　　Its virtues to tell,
When O'Hara's own chaplain
　　Has said, saying well,—
'Turlough, bold son of Brian,
　　Sit ye down, boy, again,
Till we drain the great cupaun
　　In another health to Kian.'

　　　　　　TURLOUGH O'CAROLAN:
　　　　　　Translated by SIR SAMUEL FERGUSON.

'Through the Open Door . . . .'

THROUGH the open door the hum of rosaries
  Came out and blended with the homing bees.
                              The trees
Heard nothing stranger than the rain or the wind
Or the birds—
But deep in their roots they knew a seed had sinned.

In the graveyard a goat was nibbling at a yew,
The cobbler's chickens with anxious looks
Were straggling home through nettles, over graves.
A young girl down a hill was driving cows
To a corner at the gable-end of a roofless house.

Cows were milked earlier,
The supper hurried,
Hens shut in,
Horses unyoked,
And three men shaving before the same mirror.

The trip of iron tips on tile
Hesitated up the middle aisle,
Heads that were bowed glanced up to see
Who could this last arrival be.

Murmur of women's voices from the porch,
Memories of relations in the graveyard.
On the stem
Of memory imaginations blossom.
                              In the dim
Corners in the side seats faces gather,
Lit up now and then by a guttering candle
And the ghost of day at the window.

A secret lover is saying
Three Hail Marys that she who knows
The ways of women will bring
Cathleen O'Hara (he names her) home to him.
Ironic fate! Cathleen herself is saying
Three Hail Marys to her who knows
The ways of men will bring
Somebody else home to her—
"O may he love me."
What is the Virgin Mary now to do?

Patrick Kavanagh.

The Spinning Wheel

MELLOW the moonlight to shine is beginning,
  Close by the window young Eileen is spinning;
Bent over the fire her blind grandmother, sitting,
Is crooning, and moaning, and drowsily knitting:—
"Eileen, achora, I hear someone tapping."
"'Tis the ivy, dear mother, against the glass flapping."
"Eily, I surely hear somebody sighing."
"'Tis the sound, mother dear, of the summer wind dying."
Merrily, cheerily, noiselessly whirring,
Swings the wheel, spins the wheel, while the foot's stirring;
Sprightly, and brightly, and airily ringing
Thrills the sweet voice of the young maiden singing.

"What's that noise that I hear at the window, I wonder?"
"'Tis the little birds chirping the holly-bush under."
"What makes you be shoving and moving your stool on,
And singing, all wrong, that old song of 'The Coolun'?"
There's a form at the casement—the form of her true love—
And he whispers, with face bent, "I'm waiting for you, love;
Get up on the stool, through the lattice step lightly,
We'll rove in the grove, while the moon's shining brightly."
Merrily, cheerily, noiselessly whirring,
Swings the wheel, spins the wheel, while the foot's stirring;
Sprightly, and brightly, and airily ringing
Thrills the sweet voice of the young maiden singing.

The maid shakes her head, on her lips lays her fingers,
Steals up from her seat—longs to go, and yet lingers;
A frightened glance turns to her drowsy grandmother,
Puts one foot on the stool, spins the wheel with the other,
Lazily, easily, swings now the wheel round,
Slowly and lowly is heard not the reel's sound;
Noiseless and light to the lattice above her
The maid steps—then leaps to the arms of her lover.
Slower—and slower—and slower the wheel swings;
Lower—and lower—and lower the reel rings;
Ere the reel and the wheel stopped their ringing and moving,
Through the grove the young lovers by moonlight are rov-
   ing.

                              JOHN FRANCIS WALLER.

Ringleted Youth of My Love

RINGLETED youth of my love,
  With thy locks bound loosely behind thee,
You passed by the road above,
But you never came in to find me;
Where were the harm for you
If you came for a little to see me,
Your kiss is a wakening dew
Were I ever so ill or so dreamy.

If I had golden store
I would make a nice little boreen,
To lead straight up to his door,
The door of the house of my stóreen;
Hoping to God not to miss
The sound of his footfall in it,
I have waited so long for his kiss
That for days I have not slept a minute.

I thought, oh my love! you were so—
As the moon is, or the sun on a fountain,
And I thought after that you were snow,
The cold snow on the top of the mountain;
And I thought after that you were more
Like God's lamp shining to find me,
Or the bright star of knowledge before,
And the star of knowledge behind me.

You promised me high-heeled shoes,
And satin and silk, my stóreen,
And to follow me, never to lose,
Though the ocean were round us roaring;
Like a bush in a gap in a wall
I am now left lonely without thee,
And this house I grow dead of, is all
That I see around or about me.

Translated by DOUGLAS HYDE.

Do You Remember That Night?

DO YOU remember that night
    That you were at the window,
    With neither hat nor gloves,
    Nor coat to shelter you;
    I reached out my hand to you,
    And you ardently grasped it,
    And I remained in converse with you
    Until the lark began to sing?

Do you remember that night
    That you and I were
    At the foot of the rowan tree,
    And the night drifting snow;
    Your head on my breast,
    And your pipe sweetly playing?
    I little thought that night
    Our ties of love would ever loosen.

O beloved of my inmost heart,
    Come some night, and soon,
    When my people are at rest,
    That we may talk together;
    My arms shall encircle you,
    While I relate my sad tale
    That it is your pleasant, soft converse
    That has deprived me of heaven.

The fire is unraked,
   The light extinguished,
   The key under the door,
   And do you softly draw it.
   My mother is asleep,
   And I am quite awake;
   My fortune is in my hand,
   And I am ready to go with you.
      Translated by EUGENE O'CURRY.

The Song of the Ghost

WHEN all were dreaming but Pastheen Power,
   A light came streaming beneath her bower,
A heavy foot at her door delayed,
A heavy hand on the latch was laid.

"Now who dare venture at this dark hour,
Unbid to enter my maiden bower?"
"Dear Pastheen, open the door to me,
And your true lover you'll surely see."

"My own true lover, so tall and brave,
Lives exiled over the angry wave."
"Your true love's body lies on the bier,
His faithful spirit is with you here."

"His look was cheerful, his voice was gay:
Your speech is fearful. your look is gray;
And sad and sunken your eye of blue,
But Patrick, Patrick, alas 'tis you."

Ere dawn was breaking she heard below
The two cocks shaking their wings to crow.
"O hush you, hush you, both red and gray,
Or you will hurry my love away."

"O hush your crowing both gray and red
Or he'll be going to join the dead;
O cease from calling his ghost to the mould,
And I'll come crowning your combs with gold."

When all were dreaming but Pastheen Power,
A light went streaming from out her bower,
And on the morrow when they awoke,
They knew that sorrow her heart had broke.
ALFRED PERCEVAL GRAVES.

Lullaby

SOFTLY now the burn is rushing,
   Every lark its song is hushing,
On the moor thick rest is falling,
Just one heather-blade is calling—
Calling, calling, lonely, lonely,
For my darling, for my only,
      Leanbhain O, Leanbhain O!

Trotting home, my dearie, dearie,
Wee black lamb comes, wearie, wearie,
Here its soft feet pit-a-patting
Quickly o'er the flowery matting,
See its brown-black eyes a-blinking—
Of its bed it's surely thinking,
      Leanbhain O, Leanbhain O!

The hens to roost wee Nora's shooing,
Brindley in the byre is mooing,
The tired-out cricket's quit its calling,
Velvet sleep on all is falling,—
Lark and cow, and sheep and starling,—
Feel it kiss our white-haired darling,
      Leanbhain O, Leanbhain O!
         SEUMAS MACMANUS.

I Lie Down With God

I LIE down with God, and may God lie down with me;
   The right hand of God under my head,
The two hands of Mary round about me,
The cross of the nine white angels,
From the back of my head
To the sole of my feet.
May I not lie with evil,
And may evil not lie with me.
Anna, mother of Mary,
Mary, mother of Christ,
Elizabeth, mother of John Baptist,
I myself beseech these three
To keep the couch free from sickness.
The tree on which Christ suffered
Be between me and the heavy-lying ———*,
And any other thing that seeks my harm.
With the will of God and the aid of the glorious Virgin.

Translated by ELEANOR HULL.

* The nightmare.

PART II
STREET SONGS AND COUNTRYSIDE
SONGS—MAINLY ANONYMOUS

Johnny, I Hardly Knew Ye

WHILE going the road to sweet Athy,
      Hurroo! hurroo!
While going the road to sweet Athy,
      Hurroo! hurroo!
While going the road to sweet Athy,
A stick in my hand and a drop in my eye,
A doleful damsel I heard cry:
  "Och, Johnny, I hardly knew ye!

  "With drums and guns, and guns and drums,
  The enemy nearly slew ye;
  My darling dear, you look so queer,
    Och, Johnny, I hardly knew ye!

"Where are your eyes that looked so mild?
      Hurroo! hurroo!
Where are your eyes that looked so mild?
      Hurroo! hurroo!
Where are your eyes that looked so mild,
When my poor heart you first beguiled?
Why did you run from me and the child?
  Och, Johnny, I hardly knew ye!
    With drums, etc.

"Where are the legs with which you run?
      Hurroo! hurroo!
Where are thy legs with which you run?
      Hurroo! hurroo!

Where are the legs with which you run
When first you went to carry a gun?
Indeed, your dancing days are done!
   Och, Johnny, I hardly knew ye!
     With drums, etc.

It grieved my heart to see you sail,
        Hurroo! hurroo!
It grieved my heart to see you sail,
        Hurroo! hurroo!
It grieved my heart to see you sail,
Though from my heart you took leg-bail;
Like a cod you're doubled up head and tail,
   Och, Johnny, I hardly knew ye!
     With drums, etc.

"You haven't an arm and you haven't a leg,
        Hurroo! hurroo!
You haven't an arm and you haven't a leg,
        Hurroo! hurroo!
You haven't an arm and you haven't a leg,
You're an eyeless, noseless, chickenless egg;
You'll have to be put with a bowl to beg:
   Och, Johnny, I hardly knew ye!
     With drums, etc.

"I'm happy for to see you home,
        Hurroo! hurroo!
I'm happy for to see you home,
        Hurroo! hurroo!
I'm happy for to see you home,
All from the Island of Sulloon;
So low in flesh, so high in bone;
   Och, Johnny, I hardly knew ye!
     With drums, etc.

"But sad it is to see you so,
        Hurroo! hurroo!
But sad it is to see you so,
        Hurroo! hurroo!

But sad it is to see you so,
And to think of you now as an object of woe,
Your Peggy'll still keep you on as her beau:
  Och, Johnny, I hardly knew ye!

    With drums and guns, and guns and drums,
    The enemy nearly slew ye;
    My darling dear, you look so queer,
      Och, Johnny, I hardly knew ye.

Nell Flaherty's Drake

MY NAME it is Nell, right candid I tell,
    And I live near a dell I ne'er will deny,
I had a large drake, the truth for to spake,
    My grandfather left me when going to die;
He was merry and sound, and would weigh twenty pound,
    The universe round would I rove for his sake.
Bad luck to the robber, be he drunken or sober,
    That murdered Nell Flaherty's beautiful drake.

His neck it was green, and rare to be seen,
    He was fit for a queen of the highest degree.
His body so white, it would you delight,
    He was fat, plump, and heavy, and brisk as a bee.
This dear little fellow, his legs they were yellow,
    He could fly like a swallow, or swim like a hake,
But some wicked habbage, to grease his white cabbage,
    Has murdered Nell Flaherty's beautiful drake!

May his pig never grunt, may his cat never hunt,
    That a ghost may him haunt in the dark of the night.
May his hens never lay, may his horse never neigh,
    May his goat fly away like an old paper kite;
May his duck never quack, may his goose be turned black
    And pull down his stack with her long yellow beak.
May the scurvy and itch never part from the britch
    Of the wretch that murdered Nell Flaherty's drake!

May his rooster ne'er crow, may his bellows not blow,
　　Nor potatoes to grow—may he never have none—
May his cradle not rock, may his chest have no lock,
　　May his wife have no frock for to shade her backbone.
That the bugs and the fleas may this wicked wretch tease,
　　And a piercing north breeze make him tremble and shake.
May a four-years'-old bug build a nest in the lug
　　Of the monster that murdered Nell Flaherty's drake.

May his pipe never smoke, may his tea-pot be broke,
　　And to add to the joke may his kettle not boil;
May he be poorly fed till the hour he is dead.
　　May he always be fed on lobscouse and fish oil.
May he swell with the gout till his grinders fall out,
　　May he roar, howl, and shout with a horrid toothache,
May his temple wear horns and his toes carry corns,
　　The wretch that murdered Nell Flaherty's drake.

May his dog yelp and howl with both hunger and cold,
　　May his wife always scold till his brains go astray.
May the curse of each hag, that ever carried a bag,
　　Light down on the wag till his head it turns gray.
May monkeys still bite him, and mad dogs affright him,
　　And every one slight him, asleep or awake.
May wasps ever gnaw him, and jackdaws ever claw him,
　　The monster that murdered Nell Flaherty's drake.

But the only good news I have to diffuse,
　　Is of Peter Hughes and Paddy McCade,
And crooked Ned Manson, and big-nosed Bob Hanson,
　　Each one had a grandson of my beautiful drake.
Oh! my bird he has dozens of nephews and cousins,
　　And one I must have, or my heart it will break.
To keep my mind easy, or else I'll run crazy,
　　And so ends the song of my beautiful drake.

Allalu Mo Wauleen

(The Beggar's Address to His Bag)

GOOD neighbors, dear, be cautious,
  And covet no man's pounds or pence.
Ambition's greedy maw shun,
And tread the path of innocence!
Dread crooked ways and cheating,
And be not like those hounds of Hell,
Like prowling wolves awaiting,
Which once upon my footsteps fell.

> An allalu mo wauleen,
> My little bag I treasured it;
> 'Twas stuffed from string to sauleen,
> A thousand times I measured it!

Should you ever reach Dungarvan,
That wretched hole of dole and sin,
Be on your sharpest guard, man,
Or the eyes out of your head they'll pin.
Since I left sweet Tipperary,
They eased me of my cherished load,
And left me light and airy,
A poor dark man upon the road!

> An allalu mo wauleen!
> No hole, no stitch, no rent in it,
> 'Twas stuffed from string to sauleen,
> My half-year's rent was pent in it.

74

A gay gold ring unbroken,
A token to a fair young maid,
Which told of love unspoken,
To one whose hopes were long delayed,
A pair of woolen hoseen,
Close knitted, without rib or seam,
And a pound of weed well-chosen,
Such as smokers taste in dream!

> An allalu mo wauleen,
> Such a store I had in it;
> 'Twas stuffed from string to sauleen,
> And nothing mean or bad in it!

Full oft in cosy corner
We'd sit beside a winter fire,
Nor envied prince or lord, or
To kingly rank did we aspire.
But twice they overhauled us,
The dark police of aspect dire,
Because they feared, Mo Chairdeas,
You held the dreaded Fenian fire!

> An allalu mo wauleen,
> My bag and me they sundered us,
> 'Twas stuffed from string to sauleen,
> My bag of bags they sundered us!

Yourself and I, mo stóreen,
At every hour of night and day,
Through road and lane and bohreen
Without complaint we made our way,
Till one sore day a carman
In pity took us from the road,
And faced us towards Dungarvan
Where mortal sin hath firm abode.

75

An allalu mo wauleen,
Without a hole or rent in it,
'Twas stuffed from string to sauleen,
My half-year's rent was pent in it!

My curses attend Dungarvan,
Her boats, her borough, and her fish,
May every woe that mars man
Come dancing down upon her dish!
For all the rogues behind you,
From Slaney's bank to Shannon's tide,
Are but poor scholars, mind you,
To the rogues you'd meet in Abbeyside!

An allalu mo wauleen,
My little bag I treasured it,
'Twas stuffed from string to sauleen,
A thousand times I measured it!

The Maid of the Sweet Brown Knowe

COME all ye lads and lassies and listen to me a while,
And I'll sing for you a verse or two will cause you all
to smile;
It's all about a young man, and I'm going to tell you now,
How he lately came a-courting of the Maid of the Sweet
Brown Knowe.

Said he, "My pretty fair maid, will you come along with me,
We'll both go off together, and married we will be;
We'll join our hands in wedlock bands, I'm speaking to you
now,
And I'll do my best endeavour for the Maid of the Sweet
Brown Knowe."

This fair and fickle young thing, she knew not what to say,
Her eyes did shine like silver bright and merrily did play;
She said, "Young man, your love subdue, for I am not ready
now,
And I'll spend another season at the foot of the Sweet
Brown Knowe.

Said he, "My pretty fair maid, how can you say so,
Look down in yonder valley where my crops do gently grow,
Look down in yonder valley where my horses and my plough
Are at their daily labour for the Maid of the Sweet Brown
Knowe."

"If they're at their daily labour, kind sir, it's not for me,
For I've heard of your behaviour, I have, indeed," she said;
"There is an Inn where you call in, I have heard the people
  say,
Where you rap and call and pay for all, and go home at the
  break of day."

"If I rap and call and pay for all, the money is all my own,
And I'll never spend your fortune, for I hear you have got
  none.
You thought you had my poor heart broke in talking with
  me now,
But I'll leave you where I found you, at the foot of the Sweet
  Brown Knowe."

I Know My Love

I KNOW my Love by his way of walking,
  And I know my love by his way of talking,
And I know my love dressed in a suit of blue,
And if my Love leaves me, what will I do?
    And still she cried, "I love him the best,
    And a troubled mind, sure, can know no rest,"
    And still she cried, "Bonny boys are few,
    And if my Love leaves me, what will I do?"

There is a dance house in Mar'dyke,
 And there my true love goes every night;
He takes a strange one upon his knee,
And don't you think, now, that vexes me?
    And still she cried, "I love him the best,
    And a troubled mind, sure, can know no rest,"
    And still she cried, "Bonny boys are few,
    And if my Love leaves me, what will I do?"

If my Love knew I could wash and wring,
If my Love knew I could weave and spin,
I would make a dress all of the finest kind,
But the want of money, sure, leaves me behind.

    And still she cried, "I love him the best,
    And a troubled mind, sure, can know no rest,"
    And still she cried, "Bonny boys are few,
    And if my Love leaves me, what will I do?"

I know my Love is an arrant rover,
I know he'll wander the wide world over,

In dear old Ireland he'll no longer tarry,
And an English one he is sure to marry.
    And still she cried, "I love him the best,
    And a troubled mind, sure, can know no rest,"
    And still she cried, "Bonny boys are few,
    And if my Love leaves me, what will I do?"

The Lambs on the Green Hills Stood Gazing on Me

THE lambs on the green hills stood gazing on me,
  And many strawberries grew round the salt sea,
And many strawberries grew round the salt sea,
And many a ship sailed the ocean.

And bride and bride's party to church they did go,
The bride she rode foremost, she bears the best show,
But I followed after with my heart full of woe,
To see my love wed to another.

The first place I saw her 'twas in the church stand,
Gold rings on her finger and love by the hand,
Says I, "My wee lassie, I will be the man
Although you are wed to another."

The next place I saw her was on the way home,
I ran on before her, not knowing where to roam,
Says I, "My wee lassie, I'll be by your side
Although you are wed to another."

The next place I saw her 'twas laid in bride's bed,
I jumped in beside her and did kiss the bride;
"Stop, stop," said the groomsman, "till I speak a word,
Will you venture your life on the point of my sword?
For courting so slowly you've lost this fair maid,
So begone, for you'll never enjoy her."

Oh, make my grave then both large, wide and deep,
And sprinkle it over with flowers so sweet,
And lay me down in it to take my last sleep,
For that's the best way to forget her.

My Love Is Like the Sun

THE winter is past,
   And the summer's come at last
And the blackbirds sing in every tree;
   The hearts of these are glad
   But my poor heart is sad,
Since my true love is absent from me.

   The rose upon the briar
   By the water running clear
Gives joy to the linnet and the bee;
   Their little hearts are blest
   But mine is not at rest,
While my true love is absent from me.

   A livery I'll wear
   And I'll comb out my hair,
And in velvet so green I'll appear,
   And straight I will repair
   To the Curragh of Kildare
For it's there I'll find tidings of my dear.

   I'll wear a cap of black
   With a frill around my neck,
Gold rings on my fingers I'll wear:
   All this I'll undertake
   For my true lover's sake,
He resides at the Curragh of Kildare.

I would not think it strange
Thus the world for to range,
If I only get tidings of my dear;
But here in Cupid's chain
If I'm bound to remain,
I would spend my whole life in despair.

My love is like the sun
That in the firmament does run,
And always proves constant and true;
But he is like the moon
That wanders up and down,
And every month is new.

All ye that are in love
And cannot it remove,
I pity the pains you endure;
For experience lets me know
That your hearts are full of woe,
And a woe that no mortal can cure.

The Nobleman's Wedding

ONCE I was at a nobleman's wedding—
  'Twas of a girl that proved unkind,
But now she begins to think of her losses
Her former true lover still runs in her mind.

"Here is the token of gold that was broken,
Seven long years, love, I have kept it for your sake
You gave to me as a true lover's token,
No longer with me, love, it shall remain."

The bride she sat at the head of the table,
The words he said she marked them right well;
To sit any longer she was not able,
And down at the bridegroom's feet she fell.

"One request I do make of you
And I hope you will grant it to me,
To lie this night in the arms of my mother,
And ever after to lie with thee."

No sooner asked than it was granted,
With tears in her eyes she went to bed,
And early, early, the very next morning
He rose and found that this young bride was dead.

He took her up in his arms so softly,
And carried her to the meadow so green,
And covered her over with green leaves and laurels,
Thinking she might come to life again.

Johnny's the Lad I Love

AS I roved out on a May morning,
  Being in the youthful spring,
I leaned my back close to the garden wall,
To hear the small birds sing.

And to hear two lovers talk, my dear,
To know what they would say,
That I might know a little of her mind
Before I would go away.

"Come sit you down, my heart," he says,
"All on this pleasant green,
It's full three-quarters of a year and more
Since together you and I have been."

"I will not sit on the grass," she said,
"Now nor any other time,
For I hear you're engaged with another maid,
And your heart is no more of mine.

"Oh, I'll not believe what an old man says,
For his days are well nigh done.
Nor will I believe what a young man says,
For he's fair to many a one.

"But I will climb a high, high tree,
And rob a wild bird's nest,
And I'll bring back whatever I do find
To the arms I love the best," she said,
"To the arms I love the best."

I Know Where I'm Going

I KNOW where I'm going,
  I know who's going with me,
I know who I love,
But the dear knows who I'll marry.

I'll have stockings of silk,
Shoes of fine green leather,
Combs to buckle my hair
And a ring for every finger.

Feather beds are soft,
Painted rooms are bonny;
But I'd leave them all
To go with my love Johnny.

Some say he's dark,
I say he's bonny,
He's the flower of them all
My handsome, coaxing Johnny.

I know where I'm going,
I know who's going with me,
I know who I love,
But the dear knows who I'll marry.

Cashel of Munster

I'D WED you without herds, without money, or rich array,
   And I'd wed you on a dewy morning at daydawn grey;
My bitter woe it is, love, that we are not far away
In Cashel town, though the bare deal board were our marriage-
   bed this day!

O, fair maid, remember the green hill side,
Remember how I hunted about the valleys wide;
Time now has worn me; my locks are turned to grey,
The year is scarce and I am poor, but send me not, love, away!

O, deem not my blood is of base strain, my girl,
O, deem not my birth was as the birth of the churl;
Marry me, and prove me, and say soon you will,
That noble blood is written on my right side still!

My purse holds no red gold, no coin of the silver white,
No herds are mine to drive through the long twilight!
But the pretty girl that would take me, all bare though I be and
   lone,
O, I'd take her with me kindly to the county Tyrone.

O, my girl I can see 'tis in trouble you are,
And, O, my girl, I see 'tis your people's reproach you bear:
"I am a girl in trouble for his sake with whom I fly,
And, O, may no other maiden know such reproach as I!"

Translated by SIR SAMUEL FERGUSON.

Lovely Mary Donnelly

OH, LOVELY Mary Donnelly, my joy, my only best
  If fifty girls were round you, I'd hardly see the rest;
Be what it may the time o' day, the place be where it will
Sweet looks o' Mary Donnelly, they bloom before me still.

Her eyes like mountain water that's flowing on a rock,
How clear they are, how dark they are! they give me many a
  shock.
Red rowans warm in sunshine and wetted with a shower,
Could ne'er express the charming lip that has me in its
  power.

Her nose is straight and handsome, her eyebrows lifted up,
Her chin is very neat and pert, and smooth like a china cup,
Her hair's the brag of Ireland, so weighty and so fine;
It's rolling down upon her neck, and gathered in a twine.

The dance o' last Whit-Monday night exceeded all before,
No pretty girl from miles about was missing from the floor;
But Mary kept the belt of love, and O but she was gay!
She danced a jig, she sung a song, that took my heart away.

When she stood up for dancing, her steps were so complete,
The music nearly killed itself to listen to her feet;
The fiddler mourned his blindness, he heard her so much
  praised,
But blessed his luck not to be deaf when once her voice she
  raised.

And evermore I'm whistling or lilting what you sung,
Your smile is always in my heart, your name beside my
tongue;
But you've as many sweethearts as you'd count on both your
hands,
And for myself there's not a thumb or little finger stands.

Oh, you're the flower o' womankind in country or in town;
The higher I exalt you, the lower I'm cast down.
If some great lord should come this way, and see your beauty
bright.
And you to be his lady, I'd own it was but right.

Oh, might we live together in a lofty palace hall,
Where joyful music rises, and where scarlet curtains fall!
Oh, might we live together in a cottage mean and small,
With sods or grass the only roof, and mud the only wall!

O lovely Mary Donnelly, your beauty's my distress,
It's far too beauteous to be mine, but I'll never wish it less.
The proudest place would fit your face, and I am poor and
low
But blessings be about you, dear, wherever you may go.

WILLIAM ALLINGHAM.

Draherin O Machree

I GRIEVE when I think on the dear happy days of my
   youth,
When all the bright dreams of this faithless world seem'd
   truth;
When I stray'd thro' the green wood, as gay as a mid-summer
   bee,
In brotherly love with my Draherin O Machree!

Together we lay in the sweet-scented meadows to rest,
Together we watch'd the gay lark as he sung o'er his nest,
Together we plucked the red fruit of the fragrant hawthorn
   tree,
And I loved as a sweetheart, my Draherin O Machree!

His form was straight as a hazel that grows in the glen,
His manners were courteous, and social, and gay amongst
   men;
His bosom was white as the lily on summer's green lea—
He's God's brightest image was Draherin O Machree!

Oh! sweet were his words as the honey that falls in the
   night,
And his young smiling face like the May-bloom was fresh,
   and as bright;
His eyes were like dew on the flower of the sweet apple
   tree;
My heart's spring and summer was Draherin O Machree!

He went to the wars when proud England united with France;
His regiment was first in the red battle-charge to advance;
But when night drew its veil o'er the gory and life-wasting
  fray,
Pale, bleeding, and cold lay my Draherin O Machree!

Now I'm left to weep, like the sorrowful bird of the night;
This earth and its pleasures no more shall afford me delight·
The dark, narrow grave is the only sad refuge for me,
Since I lost my heart's darling—my Draherin O Machree!

The Oul' Grey Mare

AT BREAK of day I chanced to stray
Where Seine's fair waters glide,
When to raise my heart, young Bonypart
Came forward for to ride.
On a field of green, with gallant mien,
He formed his men in square,
And down the line, with looks divine,
He rode the Oul' Grey Mare!

"My sporting boys that's tall and straight,
Take counsel and be wise;
Attintion pay to what I say,
My counsels don't despise;
Let patience guide yous everywhere,
And from traitors now beware,
For none but min that's sound within
Can ride my Oul' Grey Mare!"

Now Bonypart on her did start—
He rode too fast, *is truagh!*
She lost a shoe at Moscow Fair,
And got lamed at Waterloo;
But wait till she is back once more
Where she'll have farrier's care,
And the very next hate, she'll win the plate,
My sportin' Oul' Grey Mare!

Down by the Glenside

DOWN by the glenside I met an old woman
   A plucking young nettles nor saw I was coming,
I listened awhile to the song she was humming:—
   "Glory O! Glory O! to the Bold Fenian Men."

"Tis fifty long years since I saw the moon beamin,'
   On strong manly forms, an' on eyes with hope gleamin,'
I see them again sure thro' all my day-dreamin,'
   Glory O! Glory O! to the Bold Fenian Men."

"When I was a girl their marchin' an' drillin'
   Awoke in the glenside sounds awesome an' thrillin,'
They loved poor old Ireland an' to die they were willin'
   Glory O! Glory O! to the Bold Fenian Men."

"Some died by the glenside, some died mid the stranger,
   And wise men have told us their cause was a failure,
But they stood by old Ireland an' never feared danger,
   Glory O! Glory O! to the Bold Fenian Men."

I passed on my way, God be praised that I met her,
   Be life long or short I shall never forget her,
We may have great men but—we'll never have better,
   Glory O! Glory O! to the Bold Fenian Men.
                                        PEADAR KEARNEY.

The Boyne Water

JULY the first, of a morning clear, one thousand six hundred and ninety,
King William did his men prepare—of thousands he had thirty—
To fight King James and all his foes, encamped near the Boyne Water;
He little feared, though two to one, their multitude to scatter.

King William called his officers, saying: "Gentlemen, mind your station,
And let your valour here be shown before this Irish nation;
My brazen walls let no man break, and your subtle foes you'll scatter,
Be sure you show them good English play as you go over the water."

Both foot and horse they marched on, intending them to batter,
But the brave Duke Schomberg he was shot as he crossed over the water.
When that King William did observe the brave Duke Schomberg falling,
He reined his horse with a heavy heart, on the Enniskillenes calling:

"What will you do for me, brave boys—see yonder men retreating?
Our enemies encouraged are, and English drums are beating."
He says, "My boys feel no dismay at the losing of one commander,
For God shall be our King this day, and I'll be general under."

Within four yards of our fore-front, before a shot was fired,
A sudden snuff they got that day, which little they desired;
For horse and man fell to the ground, and some hung on their saddle:
Others turned up their forked ends, which we call coup de ladle.

Prince Eugene's regiment was the next, on our right hand advanced
Into a field of standing wheat, where Irish horses pranced;
But the brandy ran so in their heads, their senses all did scatter,
They little thought to leave their bones that day at the Boyne Water.

Both men and horse lay on the ground, and many there lay bleeding,
I saw no sickles there that day—but, sure, there was sharp shearing.
Now, praise God, all true Protestants, and heaven's and earth's Creator,
For the deliverance he sent our enemies to scatter.
The Church's foes will pine away, like churlish-hearted Nabal,
For our deliverer came this day like the great Zorobabal.

So praise God, all true Protestants, and I will say no further,
But had the Papists gained that day, there would have been
open murder.
Although King James and many more were ne'er that way
inclined,
It was not in their power to stop what the rabble they designed.

The Shan Van Vocht

OH! the French are on the say,
    Says the Shan Van Vocht;
The French are on the say,
    Says the Shan Van Vocht;
Oh! the French are in the Bay,
They'll be here without delay,
And the Orange will decay,
    Says the Shan Van Vocht.
Oh! the French are in the Bay,
They'll be here by break of day
And the Orange will decay,
    Says the Shan Van Vocht.

And where will they have their camp?
    Says the Shan Van Vocht;
Where will they have their camp?
    Says the Shan Van Vocht;
On the Curragh of Kildare,
The boys they will be there,
With their pikes in good repair,
    Says the Shan Van Vocht.
To the Curragh of Kildare
The boys they will repair
And Lord Edward will be there,
    Says the Shan Van Vocht.

Then what will the yeomen do?
        Says the Shan Van Vocht;
What should the yeomen do,
        Says the Shan Van Vocht;
What should the yeomen do,
But throw off the red and blue,
And swear that they'll be true
        To the Shan Van Vocht?
What should the yeomen do,
        But throw off the red and blue,
And swear that they'll be true
        To the Shan Van Vocht?

And what colour will they wear?
        Says the Shan Van Vocht;
What colour will they wear?
        Says the Shan Van Vocht;
What colours should be seen
Where their father's homes have been
But their own immortal green?
        Says the Shan Van Vocht.

And will Ireland then be free?
        Says the Shan Van Vocht;
Will Ireland then be free?
        Says the Shan Van Vocht;
Yes! Ireland shall be free,
From the centre to the sea;
Then hurrah for Liberty!
        Says the Shan Van Vocht.
Yes! Ireland shall be free,
From the centre to the sea;
Then hurrah for Liberty!
        Says the Shan Van Vocht.

The Wearin' o' the Green

OH, Paddy dear! and did ye hear the news that's goin'
   round?
The shamrock is forbid by law to grow on Irish ground!
No more St. Patrick's day we'll keep; his colour can't be
   seen,
For there's a cruel law ag'in' the Wearin' o' the Green!

I met with Napper Tandy, and he took me by the hand,
And he said, "How's poor ould Ireland, and how does she
   stand?"
"She's the most distressful country that ever yet was seen,
For they're hanging men and women there for the Wearin'
   o' the Green.

An' if the colour we must wear is England's cruel red,
Let it remind us of the blood that Ireland has shed;
Then pull the shamrock from your hat, and throw it on the
   sod,
An' never fear, 'twill take root there, though under foot 'tis
   trod.

When law can stop the blades of grass from growin' as they
   grow,
An' when the leaves in summer time their colour dare not
   show,
Then I will change the colour, too, I wear in my caubeen;
But till that day, plaise God, I'll stick to the Wearin' o' the
   Green.

The Rising of the Moon

"OH, THEN tell me, Shawn O'Farrall,
Tell me why you hurry so?"
"Hush, ma bouchal, hush and listen;"
And his cheeks were all a-glow:
"I bear orders from the Captain—
Get you ready quick and soon;
For the pikes must be together
At the Rising of the Moon."

"Oh, then tell me, Shawn O'Farrall
Where the gathering is to be?"
"In the oul' spot by the river
Right well known to you and me;
One word more—for signal token
Whistle up the marching tune,
With your pike upon your shoulder,
At the Rising of the Moon."

Out from many a mud-wall cabin
Eyes were watching through the night:
Many a manly chest was throbbing
For the blessed warning light;
Murmurs passed along the valley
Like the Banshee's lonely croon,
And a thousand blades were flashing
At the Rising of the Moon.

There, beside the singing river,
That dark mass of men were seen—
Far above the shining weapons
Hung their own beloved green.
Death to every foe and traitor!
Forward! strike the marching tune,
And hurrah, my boys, for freedom!
'Tis the Rising of the Moon."

Well they fought for poor Old Ireland,
And full bitter was their fate;
(Oh! what glorious pride and sorrow
Fill the name of Ninety-Eight!)
Yet, thank God, e'en still are beating
Hearts in manhood's burning noon,
Who would follow in their footsteps
At the Rising of the Moon.

The Croppy Boy

IT WAS early, early in the spring,
  The birds did whistle and sweetly sing,
Changing their notes from tree to tree,
And the song they sang was Old Ireland free.

It was early, early in the night,
The yeoman cavalry gave me a fright;
The yeoman cavalry was my downfall
And taken was I by Lord Cornwall.

'Twas in the guard-house where I was laid
And in a parlor where I was tried;
My sentence passed and my courage low
When to Dungannon I was forced to go.

As I was passing by my father's door,
My brother William stood at the door;
My aged father stood at the door,
And my tender mother her hair she tore.

As I was walking up Wexford Street
My own first cousin I chanced to meet;
My own first cousin did me betray,
And for one bare guinea swore my life away.

My sister Mary heard the express,
She ran upstairs in her morning-dress—
Five hundred guineas I will lay down,
To see my brother safe in Wexford Town.

As I was walking up Wexford Hill,
Who could blame me to cry my fill?
I looked behind and I looked before,
But my tender mother I shall ne'er see more.

As I was mounted on the platform high,
My aged father was standing by;
My aged father did me deny,
And the name he gave me was the Croppy
Boy.

It was in Dungannon this young man died,
And in Dungannon his body lies;
And you good Christians that do pass by
Just drop a tear for the Croppy Boy.

By Memory Inspired

BY Memory inspired,
And love of country fired,
The deeds of men I love to dwell upon;
And the patriotic glow
Of my spirits must bestow
A tribute to O'Connell that is gone, boys—gone:
Here's a memory to the friends that are gone!

In October Ninety-seven—
May his soul find rest in Heaven—
William Orr to execution was led on:
The jury, drunk, agreed
That Irish was his creed;
For perjury and threats drove them on, boys—on:
Here's the memory of John Mitchell that is gone!

In Ninety-eight—the month July—
The informer's pay was high;
When Reynolds gave the gallows brave MacCann;
But MacCann was Reynolds' first—
One could not allay his thirst;
So he brought up Bond and Byrne, that are gone, boys—gone:
Here's the memory of the friends that are gone!

We saw a nation's tears
Shed for John and Henry Shears;
Betrayed by Judas, Captain Armstrong;
We may forgive, but yet
We never can forget
The poisoning of Maguire that is gone, boys—gone:
Our high Star and true Apostle that is gone!

How did Lord Edward die?
Like a man, without a sigh;
But he left his handiwork on Major Swan!
But Sirr, with steel-clad breast,
And coward heart at best,
Left us cause to mourn Lord Edward that is gone, boys—
gone:
Here's the memory of our friends that are gone!

September, Eighteen-three,
Closed this cruel history,
When Emmet's blood the scaffold flowed upon:
Oh, had their spirits been wise,
They might then realise
Their freedom, but we drink to Mitchell that is gone. boys—
gone:
Here's the memory of the friends that are gone!

PART III
THE CELTIC WORLD AND THE REALM OF FAERY

Aimirgin's Invocation

I INVOKE the land of Ireland:
  Much-coursed be the fertile sea,
Fertile be the fruit-strewn mountain,
Fruit-strewn be the showery wood,
Showery be the river of waterfalls,
Of waterfalls be the lake of deep pools,
Deep-pooled be the hill-top wall,
A well of tribes be the assembly,
An assembly of kings be Temair,
Temair be the hill of the tribes,
The tribes of the sons of Mil,
Of Mil of the ships, the barks!

Let the lofty bark be Ireland,
Lofty Ireland, darkly sung,
An incantation of great cunning:
The great cunning of the wives of Bres,
The wives of Bres, of Buaigne;
The great lady, Ireland,
Eremon hath conquered her,
  I, Eber, have invoked for her.
I invoke the land of Ireland!
  Translated by PROFESSOR MAC NEILL.

St. Patrick's Breastplate

I ARISE to-day
   Through the strength of heaven:
Light of sun,
Radiance of moon,
Splendor of fire,
Speed of lightning,
Swiftness of wind,
Depth of sea,
Stability of earth,
Firmness of rock.

I arise to-day
Through God's strength to pilot me:
God's might to uphold me,
God's wisdom to guide me,
God's eye to look before me,
God's ear to hear me,
God's word to speak for me,
God's hand to guard me,
God's way to lie before me,
God's shield to protect me,
God's host to save me
From snares of devils,
From temptations of vices,
From every one who shall wish me ill,
Afar and anear,
Alone and in a multitude.

Christ to shield me to-day
Against poison, against burning,
Against drowning, against wounding,
So that there may come to me abundance of reward.
Christ with me, Christ before me, Christ behind me,
Christ in me, Christ beneath me, Christ above me,
Christ on my right, Christ on my left,
Christ when I lie down, Christ when I sit down, Christ when
     I arise,
Christ in the heart of every man who thinks of me,
Christ in the mouth of every one who speaks of me,
Christ in every eye that sees me,
Christ in every ear that hears me.

I arise to-day
Through a mighty strength, the invocation of the Trinity,
Through belief in the threeness,
Through confession of the oneness
Of the Creator of Creation.

Translated by KUNO MEYER.

111

In Praise of May

Ascribed to Fionn mac Cumhaill.

MAY-DAY! delightful day!
  Bright colours play the vale along.
Now wakes at morning's slender ray
Wild and gay the blackbird's song.

Now comes the bird of dusty hue,
The loud cuckoo, the summer-lover;
Branchy trees are thick with leaves;
The bitter, evil time is over.

Swift horses gather nigh
Where half dry the river goes;
Tufted heather clothes the height;
Weak and white the bogdown blows.

Corncrake sings from eve to morn,
Deep in corn, a strenuous bard!
Sings the virgin waterfall,
White and tall, her one sweet word.

Loaded bees with puny power
Goodly flower-harvest win;
Cattle roam with muddy flanks;
Busy ants go out and in.

Through the wild harp of the wood
Making music roars the gale—
Now it settles without motion,
On the ocean sleeps the sail.

Men grow mighty in the May,
Proud and gay the maidens grow;
Fair is every wooded height;
Fair and bright the plain below.

A bright shaft has smit the streams,
With gold gleams the water-flag;
Leaps the fish, and on the hills
Ardor thrills the leaping stag.

Loudly carols the lark on high,
Small and shy, his tireless lay,
Singing in wildest, merriest mood,
Delicate-hued, delightful May.

Translated by T. W. ROLLESTON.

The Sleep-Song of Grainne Over Dermuid

When fleeing from Fionn Mac Cumhaill

SLEEP a little, a little little, thou needst feel no fear or
dread,
Youth to whom my love is given, I am watching near thy
head.

Sleep a little, with my blessing, Dermuid of the lightsome eye,
I will guard thee as thou dreamest, none shall harm while I
am by.

Sleep, O little lamb, whose homeland was the country of the
lakes,
In whose bosom torrents tremble, from whose sides the river
breaks.

Sleep, as slept the ancient poet, Dedach, minstrel of the
South,
When he snatched from Conall Cernach Eithne of the laugh-
ing mouth.

Sleep as slept the comely Finncha 'neath the falls of Assaroe,
Who, when stately Slaine sought him, laid the Hard-head
Failbe low.

Sleep in joy, as slept fair Aine, Gailan's daughter of the
west,
Where, amid the flaming torches, she and Duvach found their
rest.

114

Sleep as Degha, who in triumph, ere the sun sang o'er the
land,
Stole the maiden he had craved for, plucked her from fierce
Deacall's hand.

Fold of Valour, sleep a little, Glory of the Western world;
I am wondering at thy beauty, marvelling how thy locks are
curled.

Like the parting of two children, bred together in one home,
Like the breaking of two spirits, if I did not see thee come.

Swirl the leaves before the tempest, moans the night-wind
o'er the lea,
Down its stony bed the streamlet hurries onward to the sea.

In the swaying boughs the linnet twitters in the darkling
light,
On the upland wastes of heather wings the grouse its heavy
flight.

In the marshland by the river sulks the otter in his den;
While the piping of the peeweet sounds across the distant
fen.

On the stormy mere the wild-duck pushes outward from the
brake,
With her downy brood beside her seeks the centre of the
lake.

In the east the restless roe-deer bellows to his frightened
hind;
On thy track the wolf-hounds gather, sniffing up against the
wind.

Yet, O Dermuid, sleep a little, this one night our fear hath
fled,
Youth to whom my love is given, see, I watch beside thy
bed.

Translated by ELEANOR HULL.

115

The Awakening of Dermuid

IN the sleepy forest where the bluebells
  Smouldered dimly through the night,
Dermuid saw the leaves like glad green waters
At daybreak flowing into light,
And exultant from his love upspringing
Strode with the sun upon the height.

Glittering on the hilltops
He saw the sunlit rain
Drift as around the spindle
A silver-threaded skein,
And the brown mist whitely breaking
Where arrowy torrents reached the plain.

A maddened moon
Leapt in his heart and whirled the crimson tide
Of his blood until it sang aloud of battle
Where the querns of dark death grind,
Till it sang and scorned in pride
Love—the froth-pale blossom of the boglands
That flutters on the waves of the wandering wind.

Flower-quiet in the rush-strewn sheiling
At the dawntime Grainne lay,
While beneath the birch-topped roof the sunlight
Groped upon its way
And stooped above her sleeping white body
With a wasp-yellow ray.

The hot breath of the day awoke her,
And wearied of its heat
She wandered out by the noisy elms
On the cool mossy peat,
Where the shadowed leaves like pecking linnets
Nodded around her feet.

She leaned and saw in the pale-grey waters,
By twisted hazel boughs,
Her lips like heavy drooping poppies
In a rich redness drowse,
Then swallow—lightly touched the ripples
Until her wet lips were
Burning as ripened rowan berries
Through the white winter air.

Lazily she lingered
    Gazing so,
As the slender osiers
Where the waters flow,
As green twigs of sally
Swaying to and fro.

Sleepy moths fluttered
In her dark eyes,
And her lips grew quieter
Than lullabies.
Swaying with the reedgrass
Over the stream
Lazily she lingered
Cradling a dream.
                AUSTIN CLARKE,
        From "The Vengeance of Finn."

The Lay of Prince Marvan

THERE is a sheeling hidden in the wood
  Unknown to all save God;
An ancient ash-tree and a hazel-bush
  Their sheltering shade afford.

Around the doorway's heather-laden porch
  Wild honeysuckles twine;
Prolific oaks, within the forest's gloom,
  Shed mast upon fat swine.

Many a sweet familiar woodland path
  Comes winding to my door;
Lowly and humble is my hermitage,
  Poor, and yet not too poor.

From the high gable-end my lady's throat
  Her trilling chant outpours,
Her sombre mantle, like the ousel's coat,
  Shows dark above my doors.

From the high oakridge where the roe-deer leaps
  The river-banks between,
Renowned Mucraime and Red Roigne's plains
  Lie wrapped in robes of green.

Here in the silence, where no care intrudes,
  I dwell at peace with God;
What gift like this hast thou to give, Prince Guaire,
  Were I to roam abroad?

The heavy branches of the green-barked yew
　　That seem to bear the sky;
The spreading oak, that shields me from the storm,
　　When winds rise high.

Like a great hostel, welcoming to all,
　　My laden apple-tree;
Low in the hedge, the modest hazel-bush
　　Drops ripest nuts for me.

Round the pure spring, that rises crystal clear,
　　Straight from the rock,
Wild goats and swine, red fox, and grazing deer,
　　At sundown flock.

The host of forest-dwellers of the soil
　　Trysting at night;
To meet them foxes come, a peaceful troop,
　　For my delight.

Like exiled princes, flocking to their home,
　　They gather round;
Beneath the river bank great salmon leap,
　　And trout abound.

Rich rowan clusters, and the dusky sloe,
　　The bitter, dark blackthorn,
Ripe whortle-berries, nuts of amber hue,
　　The cup-enclosed acorn.

A clutch of eggs, sweet honey, mead and ale,
　　God's goodness still bestows;
Red apples, and the fruitage of the heath,
　　His constant mercy shows.

The goodly tangle of the briar-trail
　　Climbs over all the hedge;
Far out of sight, the trembling waters wail
　　Through rustling rush and sedge.

Luxuriant summer spreads its coloured cloak
  And covers all the land;
Bright blue-bells, sunk in woods of russet oak,
  Their blooms expand.

The movements of the bright red-breasted wren,
  A lovely melody!
Above my house, the thrush and cuckoo's strain
  A chorus wakes for me.

The little music-makers of the world
  Chafers and bees,
Drone answer to the tumbling torrent's roar
  Beneath the trees.

From gable-ends, from every branch and stem,
  Sounds sweetest music now;
Unseen, in restless flight, the lively wren
  Flits 'neath the hazel-bough.

Deep in the firmament the sea-gulls fly,
  One widely-circling wreath;
The cheerful cuckoo's call, the poult's reply,
  Sound o'er the distant heath.

The lowing of the calves in summer-time,
  Best season of the year!
Across the fertile plain, pleasant the sound,
  Their call I hear.

Voice of the wind against the branchy wood
  Upon the deep blue sky;
Most musical the ceaseless waterfall,
  The swan's shrill cry.

No hired chorus, trained to praise its chief,
  Comes welling up for me;
The music made for Christ the Ever-young,
  Sounds forth without a fee.

Though great thy wealth, Prince Guaire, happier live
  Those who can boast no hoard;
Who take at Christ's hand that which He doth give
  As their award.

Far from life's tumult and the din of strife
  I dwell with Him in peace,
Content and grateful, for Thy gifts, High Prince,
  Daily increase.

(GUAIRE replies)

Wisely thou choosest, Marvan; I a king
  Would lay my kingdom by,
With Colman's glorious heritage I'd part
  To bear thee company!
    Translated by ELEANOR HULL.

The Counsels of O'Riordan, the Rann Maker

THE choirs of Heaven are tokened in a harp-string,
  A pigeon's egg is as crafty as the stars.
My heart is shaken by the crying of the lap-wing,
And yet the world is full of foolish wars.

There's gold on the whin-bush every summer morning.
There's struggling discourse in the grunting of a pig:
Yet churls will be scheming, and churls will be scorning,
And half the dim world is ruled by thimble-rig.

The luck of God is in two strangers meeting,
But the gates of Hell are in the city street
For him whose soul is not in his own keeping
And love a silver string upon his feet.

My heart is the seed of time, my veins are star-dust,
My spirit is the axle of God's dream.
Why should my august soul be worn or care-tost? . . .
Lo, God is but a lamp, and I his gleam.

There's little to be known, and that not kindly,
But an ant will burrow through a two-foot wall;
There's nothing rises up or falls down blindly:
That's a poor share of wisdom, but it's all.

                                          T. D. O'BOLGER.

My Love, Oh, She Is My Love

SHE casts a spell, oh, casts a spell!
  Which haunts me more than I can tell.
Dearer, because she makes me ill
Than who would will to make me well.

She is my store! oh, she my store!
Whose grey eye wounded me so sore,
Who will not place in mine her palm,
Nor love, nor calm me any more.

She is my pet, oh, she my pet!
Whom I can never more forget;
Who would not lose by me one moan,
Nor stone upon my cairn set.

She is my roon, oh, she my roon!
Who tells me nothing, leaves me soon;
Who would not lose by me one sigh,
Were death and I within one room.

She is my dear, oh, she my dear!
Who cares not whether I be here.
Who will not weep when I am dead,
But makes me shed the silent tear.

Hard my case, oh, hard my case!
For in her eye no hope I trace,
She will not hear me any more,
But I adore her silent face.

She is my choice, oh, she my choice!
Who never made me to rejoice;
Who caused my heart to ache so oft,
Who put no softness in her voice.

Great my grief, oh, great my grief!
Neglected, scorned beyond belief,
By her who looks at me askance,
By her who grants me no relief.

She's my desire, oh, my desire!
More glorious than the bright sun's fire;
Who were than wild-blown ice more cold
Were I so bold as to sit by her.

She it is who stole my heart,
And left a void and aching smart;
But if she soften not her eye,
I know that life and I must part.

     Translated by Douglas Hyde.

Aoibhinn, a leabhráin, do thriall

DELIGHTFUL, book, your trip
   to her of the ringlet head,
a pity it's not you
that's pining, I that sped.

To go, book, where she is
delightful trip in sooth!
the bright mouth red as blood
you'll see, and the white tooth.

You'll see that eye that's grey
the docile palm as well,
with all that beauty you
(not I, alas) will dwell.

You'll see the eyebrow fine
the perfect throat's smooth gleam,
and the sparkling cheek I saw
latterly in a dream.

The lithe good snow-white waist
that won mad love from me—
the handwhite swift neat foot—
these in their grace you'll see

The soft enchanting voice
that made me each day pine
you'll hear, and well for you—
would that your lot were mine.
      Translated by FLANN O'BRIEN.

The Woman of Beare

EBBING, the wave of the sea
    Leaves, where it wantoned before
Wan and naked the shore,
Heavy the clotted weed.
And my heart, woe is me!
Ebbs a wave of the sea.

I am the woman of Beare.
Foul am I that was fair,
Gold-embroidered smocks I had,
Now in rags am hardly clad.

Arms, now so poor and thin,
Staring bone and shrunken skin,
Once were lustrous, once caressed
Chiefs and warriors to their rest.

Not the sage's power, nor lone
Splendour of an aged throne,
Wealth I envy not, nor state.
Only women folk I hate.

On your heads, while I am cold,
Shines the sun of living gold
Flowers shall wreathe your necks in May:
For me, every month is grey.

Yours the bloom: but ours the fire,
Even out of dead desire.
Wealth, not men, ye love; but when
Life was in us, we loved men.

Fair the men, and wild the manes
Of their coursers on the plains;
Wild the chariots rocked, when we
Raced by them for mastery.

Lone is Femen: vacant, bare
Stands in Bregon Ronan's chair.
And the slow tooth of the sky
Frets the stones where my dead lie.

The wave of the great sea talks;
Through the forest winter stalks;
Not to-day by wood and sea
Comes King Diarmuid here to me.

I know what my King does.
Through the shivering reeds, across
Fords no mortal strength may breast,
He rows—to how chill a rest!

Amen, Time ends all.
Every acorn has to fall.
Bright at feasts the candles were,
Dark is here the house of prayer.

I, that when the hour was mine
Drank with kings the mead and wine,
Drink whey-water now, in rags
Praying among shrivelled hags.

Amen, let my drink be whey,
Let me do God's will all day—
And, as upon God I call,
Turn my blood to angry gall.

Ebb, flood, and ebb: I know
Well the ebb, and well the flow,
And the second ebb, all three—
Have they not come home to me!

Came the flood that had for waves
Monarchs, mad to be my slaves,
Crested as by foam with bounds
Of wild steeds and leaping hounds.

Comes no more that flooding tide
To my silent dark fireside.
Guests are many in my hall,
But a hand has touched· them all.

Well is with the isle that feels
How the ocean backward steals:
But to me my ebbing blood
Brings again no forward flood.

Ebbing, the wave of the sea
Leaves, where it wantoned before,
Changed past knowing the shore,
Lean and lonely and grey.
And far and farther from me
Ebbs the wave of the sea.

    Translated by STEPHEN GWYNN.

Cuchullain's Lament Over Fardiad

PLAY was each, pleasure each,
   Until Fardiad faced the beach;
One had been our student life,
One in strife of school our place,
One our gentle teacher's grace
      Loved o'er all and each.

Play was each, pleasure each,
Until Fardiad faced the beach;
One had been our wonted ways,
One the praise for feat of fields,
Scatach gave two victor-shields
      Equal prize to each.

Play was each, pleasure each,
Till Fardiad faced the beach;
Dear that pillar of pure gold
Who fell cold beside the ford,
Hosts of heroes felt his sword
      First in battle's breach.

Play was each, pleasure each,
Till Fardiad faced the beach;
Lion fiery, fierce, and bright,
Wave whose might no thing withstands,
Sweeping with the shrieking sands
      Horror o'er the beach.

Play was each, pleasure each,
Till Fardiad faced the beach;
Loved Fardiad, dear to me!
I shall dree his death for aye!
Yesterday a Mountain he—
      But a shade to-day!

Translated by DR. GEORGE SIGERSON.

King Cahal Mór of the Wine-Red Hand

I WALKED entranced
   Through a land of Morn:
The sun, with wondrous excess of light,
Shone down and glanced
Over seas of corn
And lustrous gardens aleft and right.
Even in the clime
Of resplendent Spain,
Beams no such sun upon such a land;
But it was the time,
'Twas in the reign,
Of Cahal Mór of the Wine-red Hand.

Anon stood nigh
By my side a man
Of princely aspect and port sublime
Him queried I—
"Oh, my Lord and Khan,
What clime is this, and what golden time?"
When he—"The clime
Is a clime to praise,
The clime is Erin's, the green and bland;
And it is the time,
These be the days,
Of Cahal Mór of the Wine-red Hand."

Then saw I thrones
And circling fires,
And a Dome rose near me, as by a spell,
Whence flowed the tones
Of silver lyres,
And many voices in wreathèd swell;

130

And their thrilling chime
Fell on mine ears
As the heavenly hymn of an angel-band—
"It is now the time
These be the years,
Of Cahal Mór of the Wine-red Hand."

I sought the hall,
And behold!—a change
From light to darkness, from joy to woe!
Kings, nobles, all,
Looked aghast and strange;
The minstrel group sate in dumbest show!
Had some great crime
Wrought this dread amaze,
This terror? None seemed to understand
'Twas then the time,
We were in the days,
Of Cahal Mór of the Wine-red Hand.

I again walked forth;
But lo! the sky
Showed flecked with blood, and an alien sun
Glared from the north,
And there stood on high,
Amid his shorn beams, a skeleton!
It was by the stream
Of the castled Maine,
One Autumn eve, in the Teuton's land,
That I dreamed this dream
Of the time and reign
Of Cahal Mór of the Wine-red Hand.
Translated by JAMES CLARENCE MANGAN.

Kincora

A H, WHERE, Kincora! is Brian the Great?
  And where is the beauty that once was thine?
Oh, where are the princes and nobles that sate
At the feasts in thy halls, and drank the red wine,
                    Where, O Kincora?

Oh, where, Kincora! are thy valorous lords?
Oh, whither, thou Hospitable! are they gone?
Oh, where are the Dalcassians of the Golden Swords?
And where are the warriors Brian led on?
                    Where, O Kincora?

And where is Murrough, the descendant of kings—
The defeater of a hundred—the daringly brave—
Who set but slight store by jewels and rings—
Who swam down the torrent and laughed at its wave?
                    Where, O Kincora?

And where is Donogh, King Brian's worthy son?
And where is Conaing, the Beautiful Chief?
And Kian, and Corc? Alas! they are gone—
They have left me this night alone with my grief!
                    Left me, Kincora!

And where are the chiefs with whom Brian went forth,
The ne'er-vanquished son of Evin the Brave,
The great King of Onaght, renowned for his worth,
And the hosts of Baskinn, from the western wave?
                    Where, O Kincora?

Oh, where is Duvlann of the Swift-footed Steeds?
And where is Kian, who was son of Molloy?
And where is King Lonergan, the fame of whose deeds
In the red battlefield no time can destroy?
                    Where, O Kincora?

And where is that youth of majestic height,
The faith-keeping Prince of the Scots?—Even he,
As wide as his fame was, as great as was his might,
Was tributary, O Kincora, to thee!
                    Thee, O Kincora!

They are gone, those heroes of royal birth,
Who plundered no churches, and broke no trust,
'Tis weary for me to be living on earth
When they, O Kincora, lie low in the dust!
                    Low, O Kincora!

Oh, never again will Princes appear,
To rival the Dalcassians of the Cleaving Swords!
I can never dream of meeting afar or anear,
In the east or the west, such heroes and lords!
                    Never, O Kincora!

Oh, dear are the images my memory calls up
Of Brian Boru!—how he never would miss
To give me at the banquet the first bright cup!
Ah! why did he heap on me honor like this?
                    Why, O Kincora?

I am MacLiag, and my home is on the Lake;
Thither often, to that palace whose beauty is fled,
Came Brian to ask me, and I went for his sake.
Oh, my grief! that I should live, and Brian be dead
                    Dead, O Kincora!
          Translated by JAMES CLARENCE MANGAN.

The Grave of Rury

CLEAR as air, the western waters
    evermore their sweet, unchanging song
Murmur in their stony channels
    round O'Conor's sepulchre in Cong.

Crownless, hopeless, here he lingered;
    year on year went by him like a dream,
While the far-off roar of conquest
    murmured faintly like the singing stream.

Here he died, and here they tombed him
    men of Fechin, chanting round his grave.
Did they know, ah! did they know it,
    what they buried by the babbling wave?

Now above the sleep of Rury
    holy things and great have passed away;
Stone by stone the stately Abbey
    falls and fades in passionless decay.

Darkly grows the quiet ivy,
    pale the broken arches glimmer through;
Dark upon the cloister-garden
    dreams the shadow of the ancient yew.

Through the roofless aisles the verdure
    flows, the meadow-sweet and fox-glove bloom.
Earth, the mother and consoler,
    winds soft arms about the lonely tomb.

Peace and holy gloom possess him,
    last of Gaelic monarchs of the Gael,
Slumbering by the young, eternal
    river-voices of the western vale.

                  T. W. ROLLESTON.

The Shadow House of Lugh

DREAM-FAIR, beside dream waters, it stands alone:
  A winged thought of Lugh made its corner stone:
A desire of his heart raised its walls on high,
And set its crystal windows to flaunt the sky.

Its doors of the white bronze are many and bright,
With wonderous carven pillars for his Love's delight,
And its roof of the blue wings, the speckled red,
Is a flaming arc of beauty above her head.

Like a mountain through mist Lugh towers high,
The fiery-forked lightning is the glance of his eye,
His countenance is noble as the Sun-god's face—
The proudest chieftain he of a proud De Danaan race.

He bides there in peace now, his wars are all done—
He gave his hand to Balor when the death gate was won,
And for the strife-scarred heroes who wander in the shade,
His door lieth open, and the rich feast is laid.

He hath no vexing memory of blood in slanting rain,
Of green spears in hedges on a battle plain;
But through the haunted quiet his Love's silver words
Blow round him swift as wing-beats of enchanted birds.

A grey haunted wind is blowing in the hall,
And stirring through the shadowy spears upon the wall,
The drinking-horn goes round from shadowy lip to lip—
And about the golden methers shadowy fingers slip.

The Star of Beauty, she who queens it there;
Diademed, and wondrous long, her yellow hair.
Her eyes are twin-moons in a rose-sweet face,
And the fragrance of her presence fills all the place.

He plays for her pleasure on his harp's gold wire
The laughter-tune that leaps along in trills of fire;
She hears the dancing feet of *Sidhe* where a white moon
    gleams,
And all her world is joy in the House of Dreams.

He plays for her soothing the Slumber-song:
Fine and faint as any dream it glides along:
She sleeps until the magic of his kiss shall rouse;
And all her world is quiet in the Shadow-house.

His days glide to night, and his nights glide to day:
With circling of the amber mead, and feasting gay;
In the yellow of her hair his dreams lie curled,
And her arms make the rim of his rainbow world.

                                      ETHNA CARBERY.

The King's Son

WHO rideth through the driving rain
  At such a headlong speed?
Naked and pale he rides amain
  Upon a naked steed.

Nor hollow nor height his going bars,
  His wet steed shines like silk,
His head is golden to the stars
  And his limbs are white as milk.

But, lo, he dwindles as the light
  That lifts from a black mere,
And, as the fair youth wanes from sight,
  The steed grows mightier.

What wizard by yon holy tree
  Mutters unto the sky
Where Macha's flame-tongued horses flee
  On hoofs of thunder by?

Ah, 'tis not holy so to ban
  The youth of kingly seed:
Ah! woe, the wasting of a man
  Who changes to a steed!

Nightly upon the Plain of Kings,
  When Macha's day is nigh,
He gallops; and the dark wind brings
  His lonely human cry.
                    THOMAS BOYD

The Fairy Host

PURE white the shields their arms upbear,
  With silver emblems rare o'ercast;
Amid blue glittering blades they go,
The horns they blow are loud of blast.

In well-instructed ranks of war
Before their Chief they proudly pace;
Coerulean spears o'er every crest—
A curly-tressed, pale-visaged race.

Beneath the flame /of their attack,
Bare and black turns every coast;
With such a terror to the fight
Flashes that mighty vengeful host.

Small wonder that their strength is great,
Since royal in estate are all,
Each hero's head a lion's fell—
A golden yellow mane lets fall.

Comely and smooth their bodies are,
Their eyes the starry blue eclipse,
The pure white crystal of their teeth
Laughs out beneath their thin red lips.

Good are they at man-slaying feats,
Melodious over meats and ale;
Of woven verse they wield the spell,
At chess-craft they excel the Gael.

                    Translated by ALFRED PERCEVAL GRAVES.

The Fairy Thorn

"GET up, our Anna dear, from the weary spinning-wheel;
  For your father's on the hill, and your mother is
    asleep;
Come up above the crags, and we'll dance a Highland reel
Around the Fairy Thorn on the steep."

At Anna Grace's door 'twas thus the maidens cried,
Three merry maidens fair in kirtles of the green;
And Anna laid the rock and the weary wheel aside,
The fairest of the four, I ween.

They're glancing through the glimmer of the quiet eve,
Away in milky wavings of neck and ankle bare;
The heavy-sliding stream in its sleepy song they leave,
And the crags in the ghostly air.

And linking hand-in-hand, and singing as they go,
The maids along the hillside have ta'en their fearless way,
Till they come to where the rowan trees in lonely beauty
    grow
Beside the Fairy Hawthorn grey.

The Hawthorn stands between the ashes tall and slim,
Like matron with her twin grand-daughters at her knee;
The rowan berries cluster o'er her low head grey and dim
In ruddy kisses sweet to see.

The merry maidens four have ranged them in a row,
Between each lovely couple a stately rowan stem,
And away in mazes wavy, like skimming birds they go,
Oh, never carolled bird like them!

139

But solemn is the silence on the silvery haze
That drinks away their voices in echoless repose,
And dreamily the evening has stilled the haunted braes,
And dreamier the gloaming grows.

And sinking one by one, like lark-notes from the sky,
When the falcon's shadow saileth across the open shaw,
Are hushed the maidens' voices, as cowering down they lie
In the flutter of their sudden awe.

For, from the air above and the grassy ground beneath,
And from the mountain-ashes and the old white-thorn be-
     tween,
A power of faint enchantment doth through their beings
     breathe,
And they sink down together on the green.

They sink together silent, and stealing side to side,
They fling their lovely arms o'er their drooping necks so
     fair,
Then vainly strive again their naked arms to hide,
For their shrinking necks again are bare.

Thus clasped and prostrate all, with their heads together
     bowed,
Soft o'er their bosoms beating—the only human sound—
They hear the silky footsteps of the silent fairy crowd
Like a river in the air gliding round.

Nor scream can any raise, nor prayer can any say,
But wild, wild the terror of the speechless three—
For they feel fair Anna Grace drawn silently away,
By whom they dare not look to see.

They feel their tresses twine with her parting locks of gold,
And the curls elastic falling, as her head withdraws.
They feel her sliding arms from their tranced arms unfold,
But they dare not look to see the cause;

For heavy on their senses the faint enchantment lies
Through all that night of anguish and perilous amaze
And neither fear nor wonder can ope their quivering eyes,
Or their limbs from the cold ground raise;

Till out of night the earth has rolled her dewy side,
With every haunted mountain and streamy vale below;
When, as the mist dissolves in the yellow morningtide,
The maidens' trance dissolveth so.

Then fly the ghastly three as swiftly as they may,
And tell their tale of sorrow to anxious friends in vain—
They pined away and died within the year and day,
And ne'er was Anna Grace seen again.

SAMUEL FERGUSON.

The Fairy Lover

IT was by yonder thorn I saw the fairy host
(O low night wind, O wind of the west!)
My love rode by, there was gold upon his brow,
And since that day I can neither eat nor rest.

I dare not pray lest I should forget his face
(O black north wind blowing cold beneath the sky!)
His face and his eyes shine between me and the sun:
If I may not be with him I would rather die.

They tell me I am cursed and I will lose my soul,
(O red wind shrieking o'er the thorn-grown dún!)
But he is my love and I go to him to-night,
Who rides when the thorn glistens white beneath the moon.

He will call my name and lift me to his breast,
(Blow soft O wind 'neath the stars of the south!)
I care not for heaven and I fear not hell
If I have but the kisses of his proud red mouth.

MOIREEN FOX.

The Warnings

I WAS milking in the meadow when I heard the Banshee
    keening:
Little birds were in the nest, lambs were on the lea,
Upon the brow o' the Fairy-hill a round gold moon was
    leaning—
She parted from the esker as the Banshee keened for me.

I was weaving by the door-post, when I heard the Death-
    watch beating:
And I signed the Cross upon me, and I spoke the Name of
    Three.
High and fair, through cloud and air, a silver moon was fleet-
    ing—
But the night began to darken as the Death-watch beat for
    me.

I was sleepless on my pillow when I heard the Dead man
    calling,
The Dead man that lies drowned at the bottom of the sea.
Down in the West, in wind and mist, a dim white moon was
    falling—
Now must I rise and go to him, the Dead who calls on me.

ALICE FURLONG.

The Love-Talker

I MET the Love-Talker one eve in the glen,
    He was handsomer than any of our handsome young
      men,
His eyes were blacker than the sloe, his voice sweeter far
Than the crooning of old Kevin's pipes beyond in Coolnagar.

I was bound for the milking with a heart fair and free—
My grief! my grief! that bitter hour drained the life from
      me;
I thought him human lover, though his lips on mine were
      cold,
And the breath of death blew keen on me within his hold.

I know not what way he came, no shadow fell behind,
But all the sighing rushes swayed beneath a faery wind
The thrush ceased its singing, a mist crept about,
We two clung together—with the world shut out.

Beyond the ghostly mist I could hear my cattle low,
The little cow from Ballina, clean as driven snow,
The dun cow from Kerry, the roan from Inisheer,
Oh, pitiful their calling—and his whispers in my ear!

His eyes were a fire; his words were a snare;
I cried my mother's name, but no help was there;
I made the blessed Sign; then he gave a dreary moan,
A wisp of cloud went floating by, and I stood alone.

Running ever through my head, is an old-time rune—
"Who meets the Love-Talker must weave her shroud soon."
My mother's face is furrowed with the salt tears that fall,
But the kind eyes of my father are the saddest sight of all.

I have spun the fleecy lint, and now my wheel is still,
The linen length is woven for my shroud fine and chill,
I shall stretch me on the bed where a happy maid I lay—
Pray for the soul of Mairé Og at dawning of the day!

ETHNA CARBERY.

The Green Hunters

THE Green Hunters went ridin';
  They swept down the night
Through hollows of shadow
An' pools of moonlight;
Their steeds' shoes of soft silver,
They blew ne'er a horn,
But trampled a highway
Among the ripe corn.

I looked from the half-door,
They never saw me,
For each one kept wavin'
A slip of a tree;
'Twas black as the yewan,
An' whiter than may.
An' red as the sally
That goes the wind's way.

The Green Hunter came ridin'
Back to Gore Wood;
Though they heard my lips movin',
I stood where I stood.
Oh, what do they call him
The one rode behind?
For my heart's in his holdin',
My mind in his mind.

FLORENCE M. WILSON.

The Others

FROM our hidden places
　　By a secret path,
We come in the moonlight
　　To the side of the green rath.

There the night through
　　We take our pleasure,
Dancing to such a measure
　　As earth never knew.

To song and dance
　　And lilt without a name,
So sweetly breathed
　　'Twould put a bird to shame.

And many a young maiden
　　Is there, of mortal birth,
Her young eyes laden
　　With dreams of earth.

And many a youth entranced
　　Moves slowly in the wildered round,
His brave lost feet enchanted,
　　With the rhythm of faery sound.

Music so forest wild
  And piercing sweet would bring
Silence on blackbirds singing
  Their best in the ear of spring.

And now they pause in their dancing,
  And look with troubled eyes,
Earth straying children
  With sudden memory wise.

They pause, and their eyes in the moonlight
  With fairy wisdom cold,
Grow dim and a thought goes fluttering
  In the hearts no longer old.

And then the dream forsakes them,
  And sighing, they turn anew,
As the whispering music takes them,
  To the dance of the elfin crew.

O many a thrush and a blackbird
  Would fall to the dewy ground,
And pine away in silence
  For envy of such a sound.

So the night through
  In our sad pleasure,
We dance to many a measure,
  That earth never knew.
                    Seumas O'Sullivan.

The Islands of the Ever Living

(To Prince Bran in his own house the Queen of the Islands of
the Ever Living came, bearing a blossoming branch, and she
chanted this lay to him.)

CRYSTAL and silver
The branch that to you I show:
'Tis from a wondrous isle—
Distant seas close it;
Glistening around it
The sea-horses hie them:
Emne of many shapes,
Of many shades, the island.

They who that island near
Mark a stone standing:
From it a music comes,
Unheard-of, enchanting.
They who that music hear
In clear tones answer—
Hosts sing in choruses
To its arising.

A folk that through ages along
Know no decaying,
No death nor sickness, nor
A voice raised in wailing.
Such games they play there—
Coracle on wave-ways
With chariot on land contends—
How swift the race is!

149

Only in Emne is
There such a marvel!—
Treason and wounding gone
And sorrow of parting!
Who to that island comes
And hears in the dawning
The birds, shall know all delight
All through the ages!

To him, down from a height,
Will come bright-clad women,
Laughing and full of mirth—
Lovely their coming!
Freshness of blossom fills
All the isle's mazes;
Crystals and dragon-stones
Are dropped in its ranges!

But all my song is not
For all who have heard me;
Only for one it is:
Bran, now bestir you!
Heeding the message brought,
In this, my word,
Seeing the branch I show,
Leave you a crowd!

(In her own house, the Queen of the Ever-living Islands chanted
this lay to Bran.)

Age-old, and yet
It bears the white blossom,
This tree wherein
Birds' songs are loud.
Hear! with the hours
The birds change their singing—
But always 'tis gladness—
Welcome their strain!

Look where the yellow-maned
Horses are speeding!
Look where the chariots
Are turning and wheeling!
Silver the chariots
On the plains yonder;
On the plains nigh us
Chariots of bronze!

And from our grounds,
Cultivated, familiar,
No sound arises
But is tuned to our ear.
Splendour of color
Is where spread the hazes;
Drops hair of crystal
From the waves' manes!

And of the many-colored
Land, Ildatach,
We dream when slumber
Takes us away.
'Tis like the cloud
That glistens above us,
A crown of splendour
On beauty's brow!

   Translated by PADRAIC COLUM.

PART IV
POEMS OF PLACE AND POEMS OF EXILE

The Triad of Things Not Decreed

HAPPY the stark bare wood on the hill of Bree!
   To its grey branch, green of the May: song after sigh:
Laughter of wings where the wind went with a cry
My sorrow! Song after sigh comes not to me.

Happy the dry wide pastures by Ahenree!
To them, in the speckled twilight, dew after drouth:
White clover, a fragrance in the dumb beast's mouth.
My sorrow! Dew after drouth comes not to me.

Happy Oilean Acla in the ample sea!
To its yellow shore, long-billowed flood after ebb:
Flash of the fish, silver in the sloak weeds' web,
My sorrow! Flood after ebb comes not to me.

ALICE FURLONG

The Starling Lake

MY SORROW that I am not by the little dún
By the lake of the starlings at Rosses under the hill,
And the larks there, singing over the fields of dew,
Or evening there and the sedges still.
For plain I see now the length of the yellow sand.
And Lissadell far off and its leafy ways,
And the holy mountain whose mighty heart
Gathers into it all the coloured days.
My sorrow that I am not by the little dún
By the lake of the starlings at evening when all is still,
And still in whispering sedges the herons stand.
'Tis there I would nestle at rest till the quivering moon
Uprose in the golden quiet over the hill.

SEUMAS O'SULLIVAN.

Bogac Bán

A WOMAN had I seen, as I rode by,
   Stacking her turf and chanting an old song;
But now her voice came to me like a cry
Wailing an old immeasurable wrong,
Riding the road thro' Bogac Bán.

Like a grey ribbon over the dark world,
Lying along the bog that rose each side,
The white road strayed upon the earth, and curled,
Staying its journey where the hills abide,
Riding the road thro' Bogac Bán.

It was not that the Night had laid her cloak
About the valley, going thro' the sky,
And yet a dimness like a distant smoke
Had fallen on the Earth as I rode by,
Riding the road thro' Bogac Bán.

Sweeping the sides of the mountains gaunt and high,
Floating about their faces in the pool,
A shadowy presence with a rustling sigh
Crept thro' the valley till the valley was full:
My horse's hoofs fell softy as on wool:
Riding the road thro' Bogac Bán.

In musical measures like an echo dim
The hoisting held its secret path unseen:
Slaibh Mór looked down on Mám, and Mám to him
Looked up, with Loch nanEan between:
Riding the road thro' Bogac Bán.

157

A new world and a new scene mixed its power
With the old world and the old scene of Earth's face
A doorway had been folded back an hour;
And silver lights fell with a secret grace
Where I endeavoured the white path to trace,
Riding the road thro' Bogac Bán.

Within my mind a sudden joy had birth,
For I had found an infinite company there:
The hosting of the companies of the earth,
The hosting of the companies of the air,
Treading the road thro' Bogac Bán.
The white, strange road thro' Bogac Bán.

DARRELL FIGGIS.

Killarney

IS THERE one desires to hear
  If within the shores of Eire
Eyes may still behold the scene
Far from Fand's enticements?

Let him seek the southern hills
And those lakes of loveliest water
Where the richest blooms of Spring
Burn to reddest Autumn:
And the clearest echo sings
Notes a goddess taught her.

Ah! 'twas very long ago,
And the words are now denied her:
But the purple hillsides know
Still the tones delightsome,
And their breasts, impassioned, glow
As were Fand beside them.

And though many an isle be fair,
Fairer still is Innisfallen,
Since the hour Cuchullain lay
In the bower enchanted.
See! the ash that waves to-day.
Fand its grandsire planted.

When from wave to mountain-top
All delight thy sense bewilders,
Thou shalt own the wonders wrought
Once by her skilled fingers,
Still, though many an age be gone,
Round Killarney lingers.

WILLIAM LARMINIE.

The Hills of Cualann

IN THE youth of summer
  The hills of Cualann
Are two golden horns,
Two breasts of childing,
Two tents of light

In the ancient winter
They are two rusted swords,
Two waves of darkness,
Two moons of ice.
                    JOSEPH CAMPBELL.

Ardan Mór

A S I was climbing Ardan Mór
From the shore of Sheelin lake,
I met the herons coming down
Before the water's wake.

And they were talking in their flight
Of dreamy ways the herons go
When all the hills are withered up
Nor any waters flow.

FRANCIS LEDWIDGE.

162

Clonmacnoise

IN a quiet water'd land, a land of roses,
    Stands Saint Kieran's city fair;
And the warriors of Erin in their famous generations
    Slumber there.

There beneath the dewy hillside sleep the noblest
    Of the clan of Conn,
Each below his stone with name in branching Ogham
    And the sacred knot thereon.

There they laid to rest the seven Kings of Tara,
    There the sons of Cairbre sleep—
Battle-banners of the Gael that in Kieran's plain of crosses
    Now their final hosting keep.

And in Clonmacnoise they laid the men of Teffia,
    And right many a lord of Breagh;
Deep the sod above Clan Creide and Clan Conaill,
    Kind in hall and fierce in fray.

Many and many a son of Conn the Hundred-fighter
    In the red earth lies at rest;
Many a blue eye of Clan Colman the turf covers,
    Many a swan-white breast.

        Translated by T. W. ROLLESTON.

The Little Waves of Breffny

THE grand road from the mountain goes shining to the sea,
   And there is traffic in it and many a horse and cart,
But the little roads of Cloonagh are dearer far to me,
And the little roads of Cloonagh go rambling through my
   heart.

A great storm from the ocean goes shouting o'er the hill,
And there is glory in it and terror on the wind,
But the haunted air of twilight is very strange and still,
And the little winds of twilight are dearer to my mind.

The great waves of the Atlantic sweep storming on their way,
Shining green and silver with the hidden herring shoal,
But the Little Waves of Breffny have drenched my heart in
   spray,
And the Little Waves of Breffny go stumbling through my
   soul.

EVA GORE-BOOTH.

Muckish Mountain (*The Pig's Back*)

LIKE a sleeping swine upon the skyline,
  Muckish, thou art shadowed out,
Grubbing up the rubble of the ages
With your broken, granite snout.

Muckish, greatest pig in Ulster's oakwoods,
Littered out of rock and fire,
Deep you thrust your mottled flanks for cooling
Underneath the peaty mire.

Long before the Gael was young in Ireland,
You were ribbed and old and grey,
Muckish, you have long outstayed his staying,
You have seen him swept away.

Muckish, you will not forget the people
Of the laughing speech and eye,
They who gave you name of Pig-back-mountain
And the Heavens for a sty!

SHANE LESLIE.

The Bog Lands

THE purple heather is the cloak
　　God gave the bogland brown,
But man has made a pall o' smoke
To hide the distant town.

Our lights are long and rich in change,
Unscreened by hill or spire,
From primrose dawn, a lovely range,
To sunset's farewell fire.

No morning bells have we to wake
Us with their monotone,
But windy calls of quail and crake
Unto our beds are blown.

The lark's wild flourish summons us
To work before the sun;
At eve the heart's lone Angelus
Blesses our labour done.

We cleave the sodden, shelving bank
In sunshine and in rain,
That men by winter-fires may thank
The wielders of the slane.

Our lot is laid beyond the crime
That sullies idle hands;
So hear we through the silent time
God speaking sweet commands.

Brave joys we have and calm delight—
For which tired wealth may sigh—
The freedom of the fields of light,
The gladness of the sky.

And we have music, oh, so quaint!
The curlew and the plover,
To tease the mind with pipings faint
No memory can recover;

The reeds that pine about the pools
In wind and windless weather;
The bees that have no singing-rules
Except to buzz together.

And prayer is here to give us sight
To see the purest ends;
Each evening through the brown-turf light
The Rosary ascends.

And all night long the cricket sings
The drowsy minutes fall,—
The only pendulum that swings
Across the crannied wall.

Then we have rest, so sweet, so good,
The quiet rest you crave;
The long, deep bogland solitude
That fits a forest's grave;

The long, strange stillness, wide and deep,
Beneath God's loving hand,
Where, wondering at the grace of sleep,
The Guardian Angels stand.
                    WILLIAM A. BYRNE.

The Bells of Shandon

WITH deep affection and recollection
    I often think of the Shandon bells,
Whose sounds so wild would, in days of childhood,
  Fling round my cradle their magic spells.
On this I ponder, where'er I wander,
    And thus grow fonder, sweet Cork, of thee,
      With thy bells of Shandon,
      That sound so grand on
The pleasant waters of the river Lee.

I have heard bells chiming full many a clime in,
  Tolling sublime in cathedral shrine;
While at a glib rate brass tongues would vibrate,
  But all their music spoke nought to thine;
For memory, dwelling on each proud swelling
    Of the belfry knelling its bold notes free,
      Made the bells of Shandon
      Sound far more grand on
The pleasant waters of the River Lee.

I have heard bells tolling "old Adrian's mole" in,
  Their thunder rolling from the Vatican,
With cymbals glorious, swinging uproarious
  In the gorgeous turrets of Notre Dame;
But thy sounds were sweeter than the dome of Peter
  Flings o'er the Tiber, pealing solemnly.
      Oh! the bells of Shandon
      Sound far more grand on
The pleasant waters of River Lee.

There's a bell in Moscow, while on tower and Kiosk, O!
  In St. Sophia the Turkman gets,
And loud in the air calls men to prayer
  From the tapering summit of tall minarets.
Such empty phantom I freely grant 'em,
  But there's an anthem more dear to me:
    'Tis the bells of Shandon,
      That sound so grand on
  The pleasant waters of the River Lee.

FRANCIS SYLVESTER MAHONY.
(Father Prout.)

Colum-Cille's Farewell to Ireland

ALAS for the voyage, O High King of Heaven,
 Enjoined upon me,
For that I on the red plain of bloody Cooldrevin
 Was present to see.

How happy the son is of Dima; no sorrow
 For him is designed,
He is having, this hour, round his own hill in Durrow,
 The wish of his mind.

The sounds of the winds in the elms, like strings of
 A harp being played,
The note of a blackbird that claps with the wings of
 Delight in the shade.

With him in Ros-Grencha the cattle are lowing
 At earliest dawn,
On the brink of the summer the pigeons are cooing
 And doves in the lawn.

Three things am I leaving behind me, the very
 Most dear that I know,
Tir-Leedach I'm leaving, and Durrow and Derry;
 Alas, I must go!

Yet my visit and feasting with Comgall have eased me
 At Cainneach's right hand,
And all but thy government, Eiré, have pleased me,
 Thou waterful land.
 Translated by DOUGLAS HYDE.

John O'Dwyer of the Glen

BLITHE the bright dawn found me,
  Rest with strength had crown'd me,
Sweet the birds sang around me
Sport was their toil.

The horn its clang was keeping,
Forth the fox was creeping,
Round each dame stood weeping,
O'er the prowler's spoil.

Hark! the foe is calling,
Fast the woods are falling,
Scenes and sights appalling
Mark the wasted soil.

War and confiscation
Curse the fallen nation;
Gloom and desolation
Shade the lost land o'er,

Chill the winds are blowing,
Death aloft is going,
Peace or hope seems growing
For our race no more.

Hark! the foe is calling,
Fast the woods are falling,
Scenes and sights appalling
Throng the blood-stained shore

Nobles once high-hearted,
From their homes have parted,
Scattered, scared, and started
By a base-born band.

171

Spots that once were cheering,
Girls beloved, endearing,
Friends from whom I'm steering,
Take this parting tear.

Translated by THOMAS FURLONG.

A Farewell to Patrick Sarsfield, Earl of Lucan

FAREWELL, O Patrick Sarsfield, may luck be on your path!
Your camp is broken up, your work is marred for years;
But you go to kindle into flame the King of France's wrath,
Though you leave sick Eire in tears—
                    Och, ochone!

May the white sun and moon rain glory on your head,
All hero as you are, and holy man of God!
To you the Saxons owe a many an hour of dread
In the land you have often trod—
                    Och, ochone!

The Son of Mary guard, and bless you to the end!
'Tis altered is the time when your legions were astir,
When at Cullen you were hailed as conqueror and friend,
And you crossed Narrow-water near Birr,—
                    Och, ochone!

I'll journey to the north, over mount, moor, and wave;
'Twas there I first beheld drawn up, in file and line,
The brilliant Irish hosts; they were bravest of the brave.
But alas, they scorned to combine—
                    Och, ochone!

I saw the royal Boyne when his billows flashed with blood
I fought at Graine Og, when a thousand horsemen fell;
On the dark empurpled plain of Aughrim, too, I stood,
On the plain by Tubberdonny's well—
                    Och, ochone!

To the heroes of Limerick, the City of the Fights,
Be my best blessing borne on the wings of the air;
We had card-playing there o'er our camp fires at night,
And the Word of Life, too, and prayer—
                              Och, ochone!

But for you, Londerderry, may plague smite and slay
Your people! May ruin desolate you stone by stone!
Through you there's many a gallant youth lies coffinless to-
    day
With the winds for mourners alone—
                              Och, ochone!

I clomb the high hill on a fair summer noon,
And saw the Saxons muster, clad in armour blinding bright:
Oh, rage withheld my hand, or gunsman and dragoon
Should have supped with Satan that night!—
                              Och, ochone!

How many a noble soldier, how many a cavalier,
Careered along this road, seven fleeting weeks ago,
With silver-hilted sword, with matchlock and with spear,
Who now, mavrone! lieth low—
                              Och, ochone!

All hail to thee, Beinn Eidir but ah, on thy brow
I see a limping soldier, who battled and who bled
Last year in the cause of the Stuart, though now
The worthy is begging his bread—
                              Och, ochone!

And Diarmid oh, Diarmid he perished in the strife;
His head it was spiked upon a halberd high;
His colours they were trampled: he had no chance of life
If the Lord God Himself stood by!—
                Och, ochone!

But most, oh my woe I lament and lament
For the ten valient heroes who dwelt nigh the Nore,
And my three blessed brothers; they left me and went
To the wars, and returned no more—
                Och, ochone!

On the bridge of the Boyne was our first overthrow;
By Slaney the next, for we battled without rest;
The third was at Aughrim. O Eire! thy woe
Is a sword in my bleeding breast—
                Och, ochone!

Oh, the roof above our heads, it was barbarously fired,
While the black Orange guns blazed and bellowed around!
And as volley followed volley, Colonel Mitchel inquired
Whether Lucan still stood his ground?—
                Och, ochone!

But O'Kelly still remains, to defy and to toil,
He has memories that hell won't permit him to forget,
And a sword that will make the blue blood flow like oil
Upon many an Aughrim yet!—
                Och, ochone!

And I never shall believe that my fatherland can fall
With the Burkes, and the Dukes, and the son of Royal James,
And Talbot, the captain, and Sarsfield above all,
The beloved of damsels and dames—
                Och, ochone!
          Translated by JAMES CLARENCE MANGAN.

Fontenoy. *1745*

I.—*Before the Battle; night.*

OH, BAD the march, the weary march, beneath these alien
skies,
But good the night, the friendly night, that soothes our tired
eyes.
And bad the war, the tedious war, that keeps us sweltering
here,
But good the hour, the friendly hour, that brings the battle
near.
That brings us on the battle, that summons to their share
The homeless troops, the banished men, the exiled sons of
Clare.

Oh, little Corca Bascinn, the wild, the bleak, the fair!
Oh, little stony pastures, whose flowers are sweet, if rare!
Oh, rough the rude Atlantic, the thunderous, the wide,
Whose kiss is like a soldier's kiss which will not be denied!
The whole night long we dream of you, and waking think
we're there,—
Vain dream, and foolish waking, we never shall see Clare.

The wind is wild to-night, there's battle in the air;
The wind is from the west, and it seems to blow from Clare.
Have you nothing, nothing for us, loud brawler of the night?
No news to warm our heart-strings, to speed us through the
fight?
In this hollow, star-pricked darkness, as in the sun's hot
glare,
In sun-tide, in star-tide, we thirst, we starve for Clare!

Hark! yonder through the darkness one distant rat-tat-tat!
The old foe stirs out there, God bless his soul for that!
The old foe musters strongly, he's coming on at last,
And Clare's Brigade may claim its own wherever blows fall
    fast.
Send us, ye western breezes, our full, our rightful share,
For Faith, and Fame, and Honour, and the ruined hearths of
    Clare.

EMILY LAWLESS.

II.—After the Battle; early dawn, Clare coast.

"MARY MOTHER, shield us! Say, what men are ye,
   Sweeping past so swiftly on this morning sea?"
"Without sails or rowlocks merrily we glide
Home to Corca Bascinn on the brimming tide."

"Jesus save you, gentry! why are you so white,
Sitting all so straight and still in this misty light?"
"Nothing ails us, brother; joyous souls are we,
Sailing home together, on the morning sea."

"Cousins, friends, and kinsfolk, children of the land,
Here we come together, a merry, rousing band;
Sailing home together from the last great fight,
Home to Clare from Fontenoy, in the morning light.

"Men of Corca Bascinn, men of Clare's Brigade,
Harken stony hills of Clare, hear the charge we made;
See us come together, singing from the fight,
Home to Corca Bascinn, in the morning light."
                                   EMILY LAWLESS.

In Spain

YOUR sky is a hard and a dazzling blue,
   Your earth and sands are a dazzling gold,
And gold or blue is the proper hue,
You say for a swordsman bold.

In the land I have left the skies are cold,
The earth is green, the rocks are bare,
Yet the devil may hold all your blue and your gold
Were I only once back there!

EMILY LAWLESS.

In Spain: Drinking Song

MANY are praised, and some are fair,
  But the fairest of all is *She,*
And he who misdoubts let him have a care,
For her liegemen sworn are we!
Then Ho! for the land that is green and **grey,**
The land of all lands the best,
For the South is bright and the East is **gay,**
But the sun shines last in the West,
            The West!
The sun shines last in the West!

A queen is she, though a queen forlorn,
A queen of tears from her birth,
Ragged and hungry, woeful and worn,
Yet the fairest Fair on the earth.

Then here's to the land that is green and **grey,**
The land of all lands the best!
For the South is bright, and the East is gay,
But the sun shines last in the West.
            The West!
The sun shines last in the West!

EMILY LAWLESS.

The Battle Eve of the Irish Brigade

THE mess-tent is full, and the glasses are set,
  And the gallant Count Thomond is president yet;
The vet'ran arose, like an uplifted lance,
Crying—"Comrades, a health to the monarch of France!"
With bumpers and cheers they have done as he bade
For King Louis is loved by the Irish Brigade.

"A health to King James," and they bent as they quaffed,
"Here's to George the Elector," and fiercely they laughed,
"Good luck to the girls we wooed long ago,
Where Shannon, and Barrow, and Blackwater flow;"
"God prosper Old Ireland,"—you'd think them afraid,
So pale grew the chiefs of the Irish Brigade.

"But surely, that light cannot be from our lamp
And that noise—are they *all* getting drunk in the camp?"
"Hurrah! boys, the morning of battle is come,
And the *generale's* beating on many a drum."
So they rush from the revel to join the parade:
For the van is the right of the Irish Brigade.

They fought as they revelled, fast, fiery and true,
And, though victors, they left on the field not a few;
And they, who survived, fought and drank as of yore,
But the land of their heart's hope they never saw more;
For in far foreign fields, from Dunkirk to Belgrade,
Lie the soldiers and chiefs of the Irish Brigade.

THOMAS DAVIS.

The Fair Hills of Ireland

A PLENTEOUS place is Ireland for hospitable cheer,
        Uileacán dubh O!
Where the wholesome fruit is bursting from the yellow barley ear;
        Uileacán dubh O!
There is honey in the trees where her misty vales expand,
And her forest paths in summer are by falling waters fanned;
There is dew at high noontide there, and springs i' the yellow
    sand,
On the fair hills of holy Ireland.

Curled he is and ringleted, and plaited to the knee,
        Uileacán dubh O!
Each captain who comes sailing across the Irish sea;
        Uileacán dubh O!
And I will make my journey, if life and health but stand
Unto that pleasant country, that fresh and fragrant strand,
And leave your boasted braveries, your wealth and high
    command,
For the fair hills of holy Ireland.

Large and profitable are the stacks upon the ground,
        Uileacán dubh O!
The butter and the cream do wonderously abound,
        Uileacán dubh O!

The cresses on the water and the sorrels are at hand,
And the cuckoo's calling daily his note of music bland
And the bold thrush sings so bravely his song i' the forests
    grand,
On the fair hills of holy Ireland.

Translated by SAMUEL FERGUSON.

The Winding Banks of Erne

ADIEU to Belashanny, where I was bred and born;
  Go where I may I'll think of you, as sure as night and
    morn:
The kindly spot, the friendly town, where every one is known,
And not a face in all the place but partly seems my own;
There's not a house or window, there's not a field or hill,
But east or west, in foreign lands, I'll recollect them still;
I leave my warm heart with you, though my back I'm forced
    to turn—
Adieu to Belashanny, and the winding banks of Erne!

No more on pleasant evenings we'll saunter down the Mall,
When the trout is rising to the fly, the salmon to the fall.
The boat comes straining on her net, and heavily she creeps,
Cast off, cast off—she feels the oars, and to her berth she
    sweeps;
Now fore and aft keep hauling, and gathering up the clew,
Till a silver wave of salmon rolls in among the crew
Then they may sit, with pipes a-lit, and many a joke and
    yarn:
Adieu to Belashanny, and the winding banks of Erne!

The music of the waterfall, the mirror of the tide ,
When all the green-hill'd harbour is full from side to side,
From Portnasun to Bulliebawns, and round the Abbey Bay,
From rocky Inis Saimer to Coolnargit sandhills grey;
While far upon the southern line, to guard it like a wall,
The Leitrim mountains clothed in blue gaze calmly over all,
And watch the ship sail up or down, the red flag at her
    stern—
Adieu to these, adieu to all the winding banks of Erne!

Farewell to you, Kildoney lads, and them that pull an oar,
A lugsail set, or haul a net, from the point to Mullaghmore;
From Killybegs to bold Slieve-League, that ocean mountain
steep,
Six hundred yards in air aloft, six hundred in the deep;
From Dooran to the Fairy Bridge, and round by Tullen
strand,
Level and long, and white with waves, where gull and curlew
stand;
Head out to sea, when on your lee the breakers you dis-
cern—
Adieu to all the billowy coast and the winding banks of
of Erne!

Farewell, Coolmore, Bundoran! and your summer crowds that
run
From inland homes to see with joy the Atlantic setting sun;
To breathe the buoyant salted air, and sport among the
waves;
To gather shells on sandy beach, and tempt the gloomy
caves;
To watch the flowing, ebbing tide, the boats, the crabs, the
fish;
Young men and maids to meet and smile, and form a tender
wish;
The sick and old in search of health, for all things have their
turn—
And I must quit my native shore and the winding banks of
Erne!

Farewell to every white cascade from the Harbour to Belleek,
And every pool where fins may rest, and ivy-shaded creek;
The sloping fields, the lofty rocks, where ash and holly
grow,
The one split yew-tree gazing on the curving flood below;
The Lough that winds through islands under Turaw moun-
tain green
And Castle Caldwell's stretching woods, with tranquil bays
between;
And Breesie Hill, and many a pond among the heath and
fern—
For I must say adieu—adieu to the winding banks of Erne!

The thrush will call through Camlin groves the live-long sum-
mer day;
The waters run by mossy cliff, and banks with wild flowers
gay;
The girls will bring their work and sing beneath a twisted
thorn,
Or stray with sweethearts down the path among the growing
corn;
Along the riverside they go, where I have often been—
O, never shall I see again the days that I have seen!
A thousand chances are to one I never may return—
Adieu to Belashanny, and the winding banks of Erne!

Adieu to evening dances, where merry neighbours meet,
And the fiddle says to boys and girls, "get up and shake
your feet!"

To shanachas and wise old talk of Erin's days gone by
Who trench'd the rath on such a hill, and where the bones may
lie
Of saint, or king, or warrior chief; with tales of fairy
power,
And tender ditties sweetly sung to pass the twilight hour.
The mournful song of exile is now for me to learn—
Adieu, my dear companions on the winding banks of Erne!

Now measure from the Commons down to each end of the
Purt,
Round the Abbey, Moy, and Knather,—I wish no one any
hurt;
The Main Street, Back Street, College Lane, the Mall and
Portnasun,
If any foes of mine are there, I pardon every one.
I hope that man and womankind will do the same by me;
For my heart is sore and heavy at voyaging the sea.
My loving friends I'll bear in mind, and often fondly turn
To think of Belashanny and the winding banks of Erne!

If ever I'm a money'd man, I mean, please God, to cast
My golden anchor in the place where youthful years were
past;
Though heads that now are black and brown must meanwhile
gather grey,
New faces rise by every hearth, and old ones drop away—
Yet dearer still that Irish hill than all the world beside;
It's home, sweet home, where'er I roam, through lands and
waters wide.
And if the Lord allows me, I surely will return
To my native Belashanny, and the winding banks of Erne!

WILLIAM ALLINGHAM.

Corrymeela

OVER here in England I'm helpin' wi' the hay,
  And I wisht I was in Ireland the livelong day;
Weary on the English hay, an' sorra take the wheat!
Och! Corrymeela, an' the blue sky over it.

There's a deep dumb river flowin' by beyont the heavy trees,
This livin' air is moithered wi' the hummin' o' the bees;
I wisht I'd hear the Claddagh burn go runnin' through the
    heat,
Past Corrymeela, wi' the blue sky over it.

The people that's in England is richer nor the Jews,
There's not the smallest young gossoon but thravels in his
    shoes!
I'd give the pipe between me teeth to see a barefut child,
Och! Corrymeela, an' the low south wind.

Here's hands so full o' money an' hearts so full o' care,
By the luck o' love! I'd still go light for all I did go bare.
"God save ye, colleen dhas," I said; the girl she thought me
    wild!
Fair Corrymeela, an' the low south wind.

D'ye mind me now, the song at night is mortial hard to
    raise,
The girls are heavy goin' here, the boys are ill to plase;
When ones't I'm out this workin' hive, 'tis I'll be back
    again—
Aye, Corrymeela, in the same soft rain.

188

The puff o' smoke from one ould roof before an English
    town!
For a *shaugh* wid Andy Feelan here I'd give a silver crown,
For a curl o' hair like Mollie's ye'll ask the like in vain,
Sweet Corrymeela, an' the same soft rain.

MOIRA O'NEILL.

The Irish Peasant Girl

SHE lived beside the Anner,
    At the foot of Slievna-man,
A gentle peasant girl,
With mild eyes like the dawn;
Her lips were dewy rosebuds;
Her teeth of pearls rare;
And a snow-drift 'neath a beechen bough
Her neck and nut-brown hair.

How pleasant 'twas to meet her
On Sunday, when the bell
Was filling with its mellow tones
Lone wood and grassy dell
And when at eve young maidens
Strayed the river bank along,
The widow's brown-haired daughter
Was loveliest of the throng.

O brave, brave Irish girls—
We well may call you brave!—
Sure the least of all your perils
Is the stormy ocean wave,
When you leave our quiet valleys,
And cross the Atlantic's foam,
To hoard your hard-won earnings
For the helpless ones at home.

"Write word to my own dear mother—
Say, we'll meet with God above;
And tell my little brothers
I send them all my love;
May the angels ever guard them,
Is their dying sister's prayer"—
And folded in a letter
Was a braid of nut-brown hair.

Ah, cold and well-nigh callous,
This weary heart has grown
For thy helpless fate, dear Ireland,
And for sorrows of my own;
Yet a tear my eye will moister,
When by Anner side I stray,
For the lily of the mountain foot
That withered far away.

CHARLES JOSEPH KICKHAM.

The County of Mayo

ON THE deck of Patrick Lynch's boat I sat in woeful
    plight,
Through my sighing all the weary day, and weeping all the
    night,
Were it not that full of sorrow from my people forth I go,
By the blessed sun! 'tis royally I'd sing thy praise, Mayo!

When I dwelt at home in plenty, and my gold did much
    abound,
In the company of fair young maids the Spanish ale went
    round—
'Tis a bitter change from those gay days that now I'm forced
    to go,
And must leave my bones in Santa Cruz, far from my own
    Mayo.

They are altered girls in Irrul now; 'tis proud they're grown
    and high,
With their hair-bags and their top-knots—for I pass their
    buckles by;
But it's little now I heed their airs, for God will have it so,
That I must depart for foreign lands, and leave my sweet
    Mayo.

'Tis my grief that Patrick Loughlinn is not Earl in Irrul still,
And that Brian Duff no longer rules as lord upon the hill,
And that Colonel Hugh MacGrady should be lying cold and
    low,
And I be sailing, sailing from the County of Mayo.

Translated by GEORGE FOX.

PART V
SATIRES AND LAMENTS

Dido to Aeneas

N̲O̲ GODDESS is thy parent, nor th'art of Dardanus offspring,
    Thou perjured faitour: but amidst rocks, Caucasus haggish
Bred thee, with a tiger's sour milk unseasoned, uddered.
What shall I dissemble? What points more weighty reserve I?
At my tears showering did he sigh? Did he wink with his eyelid?
Once did he weep vanquished? Did he yield once mercy to
    lovemate?
What shall I first utter? Will not grand Juno with hastening?
Nor the father Saturn with his eyes bent rightly behold this?
Faith quite is exiled: from the shore late a runagate hedgebrat,
A tarbreech quystroun did I take, with frenzy betrashed
I placed in kingdom, both ships and company gracing.
Woe to me thus stamping, such brainsick foolery belching.
Mark the speech, I pray you, well couched: now soothtell Apollo,
Now Lycian's fortunes, from very Jupiter heavenly
A menacing message by the God's ambassador uttered.
Forsooth: this thy viadge with care Saints celical heapeth,
Their brains unquieted with this baldare be buzzing.
I stay not thy body, nor on baw vaw trumpery descant.
Pack to soil Italian; cross the seas; fish for a kingdom.
Verily, in hope rest I (if gods may take duly revengement)
With gagd rocks compassed, then vainly "Dido" reciting
Thou shalt be punished. I'll with fire swartish hop after.
When death hath untwined my soul from carcase his holding,
I will, as hobgoblin, follow thee: thou shalt be sore handled.
I shall hear, I doubt not, thy pangs in Limbo related.
RICHARD STANIHURST.

On Himself

ON RAINY days alone I dine
 Upon a chick and pint of wine.
On rainy days I dine alone
And pick my chicken to the bone;
But this my servants much enrages,
No scraps remain to save board-wages.
In weather fine I nothing spend,
But often spunge upon a friend;
Yet, where he's not so rich as I,
I pay my club, and so good-bye.
                    JONATHAN SWIFT.

On *An Ill-Managed House*

LET me thy properties explain:
 A rotten cabin dropping rain:
Chimneys, with scorn rejecting smoke;
Stools, tables, chairs, and bedsteads broke.
Here elements have lost their uses,
Air ripens not, nor earth produces:
In vain we make poor Sheelah toil,
Fire will not roast, nor water boil.
Through all the valleys, hills, and plains,
The Goddess Want, in triumph reigns:
And her chief officers of state,
Sloth, Dirt, and Theft, around her wait.
                    JONATHAN SWIFT.

On the World

WITH a whirl of thoughts oppress'd,
    I sunk from reverie to rest.
A horrid vision seized my head,
I saw the graves give up their dead!
Jove, arm'd with terrors, bursts the skies,
And thunder roars and lightning flies!
Amazed, confused, its fate unknown,
The world stands trembling at his throne!
While each pale sinner hung his head,
Jove, nodding, shook the heavens, and said:
"Offending race of human kind,
By nature, reason, learning, blind;
You who, through frailty, stepp'd aside;
And you, who never fell from pride:
You who in different sects were shamm'd,
And come to see each other damn'd;
(So some folk told you, but they knew
No more of Jove's designs than you;)
—The world's mad business now is o'er,
And I resent these pranks no more.
—I to such blockheads set my wit!
I damn such fools!—Go, go, you're bit."
JONATHAN SWIFT.

Righteous Anger

THE lanky hank of a she in the inn over there
   Nearly killed me for asking the loan of a glass of beer:
May the devil grip the whey-faced slut by the hair,
And beat bad manners out of her skin for a year.

That parboiled imp, with the hardest jaw you will see
On virtue's path, and a voice that would rasp the dead,
Came roaring and raging the minute she looked on me,
And threw me out of the house on the back of my head!

If I asked her master he'd give me a cask a day;
But she, with the beer at hand, not a gill would arrange!
May she marry a ghost and bear him a kitten, and may
The High King of Glory permit her to get the mange.

JAMES STEPHENS.
From the Irish of David O'Bruaidar.

The Petition of Tom Dermody to the Three Fates in Council Sitting

RIGHT rigorous, and so forth! Humbled
    By cares and mourning, tost and tumbled,
Before your Ladyships, Tom Fool,
Knowing above the rest you rule,
Most lamentably sets his case
With a bold heart and saucy face.
Sans shoes or stockings, coat or breeches,
You see him now, most mighty witches,
His body worn like an old farthing,
The angry spirit just a-parting,
His credit rotten, and his purse
As empty as a cobbler's curse;
His Poems, too, unsold—that's worse!
In short, between confounded crosses,
Patrons all vexed and former losses,
Sure as a gun he cannot fail,
Next week to warble in a jail,
Which jail to folks not very sanguine
Is just as good or worse than hanging;
Though in the first vain hopes flatter,
But Hope's quite strangled by the latter.
Thus is a poor rhyming rascal treated,
Fairly, or rather fouly cheated
Of all the goods from wit accruing,
(Wit that's synonomous with ruin).
Then take it in your head-piece, Ladies,

To set up a poor Bard, whose trade is
Low fallen enough in conscience; pity
The maker of this magic ditty;
And turn your Wheel once more in haste
To see him on the summit placed,
For well you wot that woes ('od rot 'em)
Have long since stretched him at the bottom,
Where he who erst fine lyrics gabbled
With mire and filth was sorely dabbled,
So pitifully pelted, that
He looks like any drowned rat.
O Justice, Justice, take his part!
O lift him on thy lofty Cart
Magnific Fame! And let fat Plenty
Marry one Poet out of Twenty!

THOMAS DERMODY.

To an Anti-poetical Priest

YOU messenger that comes from Rome,
  The place whence bulls and sermons come
Against our poets you appeal;
Well, show your writing and your seal.
Come, priest, display your written ban;
From Peter's heir, that holy man;
If 'tis too sacred to be shown,
Then make its general purport known.
We've stood your sermons long enough;
We want the authentic Roman stuff,
And even if you change your tone,
There's harm enough already done.
Rome never made your silly rules.
What, banish all the bardic schools?
Such mouldy style, such lore unsound
On Roman soil were never found.
Well, can't the document be shown,
That shall our royal art unthrone?
Come, Cleric, and obey our call!
Come, out with your encyclical!
Words decent author never wrote,
And turgid stuff, not worth a groat,
Low English learning, misapplied
Against our bards, our country's pride!
In learned books sweet poetry
Is 'Donum Dei' frequently,
And if the sense of this we sift,
'Tis very clear it means 'God's Gift.'
If 'tis forbid to pay for lays,
And good men are debarred from praise,
Why, then, perhaps, it does not matter
If scoundrels are immune from satire.
If this decree you do intend
To serve some economic end,
No one will starve, my reverend man,
For lack of your peculiar ban.
'Tis strange that when Saint Patrick came
From Rome he did not do the same,
And ban from Ireland ever more
The arts that were her joy before.
And Columcille would ne'er deny

201

Reward to verse that told no lie;
What could have made him so remiss,
If there be any truth in this?
From grassy Fodhla once before
The bards were sent to exile sore;
But Columcille, who held them dear,
Reversed their doom within a year.
'Tis said that at a bard's complaint
The holy statue of a Saint
Lent that presumptuous rogue a shoe;
There's nothing poetry cannot do!
The prize that can be given by none
I'll win from Blessed Mary's Son,
And if there's truth in what they tell
I'll get to Heaven for writing well.
The praise of men may rise and fall,
Then praise the Lord that made them all,
And when all earthly praise grows dim,
There's still the joy of praising Him.
By Him were all our blessings given,
Then praise the King of Highest Heaven!
Let land and sea alike proclaim
His noble acts and praise His Name!
Tho' verses be but vanity,
They have their own eternity,
And vain enough, when all is said,
The men for whom the verse is made!
And he that is to poets cold
Gains not thereby more steeds or gold,
And he that ne'er a verse can rouse,
Owns but till death his bulls and cows.
If verse expired, good gentlemen,
Where were your lays and histories then?
You'd know your sires but could not track
Your families much further back.
And were our fount of knowledge dry,
Who could to men of rank supply
The branches of their pedigree,
And Gaelic geneology?
What consequences would ensue
To gallant knights, the like of you,
Who could not, if no poet sang,
Detect the roots from which you sprang?

Unknown were skirmish, raid and fight,
Unknown the feats of bravest knight,
When once his valient deeds were done,
Each king and royal house unknown.
Tho' Guaire died he liveth yet
And who Cuchulain shall forget?
The Red Branch Hall is honored still,
And Brian lives and ever will.
They perish not who praised are;
Is Conall dead or Concobar?
They have not passed from Fodhla's plains,
And Fergus yet with us remains.
And Lugh that fell before MacCuill,
No bone of him remaineth still,
And yet so bright his fame appears
'Twill keep him deathless through the years.
The good, the valiant and the strong,
Their deeds survive in bardic song,
Or swift oblivion's shroud would fall
On Niall and Cormac, Conn and all.
You Kings that rule in hall and fort,
The poets shall your stock support;
In north or south or east or west,
'Tis they uphold your house the best.
If there be not a voice to sing,
With lute and harp accompanying,
The glorious feats of men of worth
Will pass for ever from the earth.
Oh, shall our nobles cease to trace
Their fathers' fame, their lordly race?
Let poets their achievements tell,
Or bid the ancient times farewell.
Did all forget what poets sing
Of ancient huntsman, warrior, king,
Nor learned of Donal or of Conn,
The bondsman and the free were one!
So, Irishmen, if this decree
Expel the bards, where shall we be?
For every Gael that shows so brave
Is nothing better than a slave!

GIOLLA BRIGHDE MACNAMEE
(*Thirteenth Century*) :
Translated by the EARL OF LONGFORD.

The Night Before Larry Was Stretched

THE night before Larry was stretched,
    The boys they all paid him a visit;
A bait in their sacks, too, they fetched;
They sweated their duds till they riz it:
For Larry was ever the lad,
When a boy was condemned to the squeezer,
Would fence all the duds that he had
To help a poor friend to a sneezer,
And warm his gob 'fore he died.

The boys they came crowding in fast,
They drew all their stools round about him,
Six glims round his trap-case were placed,
He couldn't be well waked without 'em.
When one of us asked could he die
Without having truly repented,
Says Larry, "That's all in my eye;
And first by the clargy invented,
To get a fat bit for themselves."

"I'm sorry, dear Larry," says I,
"To see you in this situation;
And blister my limbs if I lie,
I'd as lieve it had been my own station."
"Ochone! it's all all over," says he,
"For the neck-cloth I'll be forced to put on,
And by this time to-morrow you'll see
Your poor Larry as dead as a mutton,
Because, why, his courage was good.

"And I'll be cut up like a pie,
And my nob from my body be parted.
"You're in the wrong box, then," says I,
"For blast me if they're so hard-hearted;
A chalk on the back of your neck
Is all that Jack Ketch dares to give you;
Then mind not such trifles a feck,
For why should the likes of them grieve you?
And now, boys, come tip us the deck."

The cards being called for, they played,
Till Larry found one of them cheated;
A dart at his napper he made
(The boy being easily heated);
"Oh, by the hokey, you thief,
I'll scuttle your nob with my daddle!
You cheat me because I'm in grief,
But soon I'll demolish your noddle,
And leave you your claret to drink."

Then the clergy came in with his book,
He spoke him so smooth and so civil;
Larry tipped him a Kilmainham look,
And pitched his big wig to the devil;
Then sighing, he threw back his head,
To get a sweet drop of the bottle,
And pitiful sighing, he said:
"Oh, the hemp will be soon round my throttle,
And choke my poor windpipe to death.

"Though sure it's the best way to die,
Oh, the devil a better a-living!
For, sure when the gallows is high
Your journey is shorter to heaven:
But what harasses Larry the most,
And makes his poor soul melancholy,
Is to think on the time when his ghost
Will come in a sheet to sweet Molly—
Oh, sure it will kill her alive!"

So moving these last words he spoke,
We all vented our tears in a shower;
For my part, I thought my heart broke,
To see him cut down like a flower.
On his travels we watched him next day,
Oh, the throttler! I thought I could kill him;
But Larry not one word did say,
Nor changed till he came to "King William"—
Then, musha! his color grew white.

When he came to the nubbling chit,
He was tucked up so neat and so pretty,
The rumbler jogged off from his feet,
And he died with his feet to the city;
He kicked, too—but that was all pride,
But soon you might see 'twas all over;
Soon after the noose was untied,
And at darky we waked him in clover,
And sent him to take a ground sweat.

Anonymous.

Bruadar and Smith and Glinn

BRUADAR and Smith and Glinn,
   Amen, dear God, I pray,
May they lie low in waves of woe,
   And tortures slow each day!
           Amen!

Bruadar and Smith and Glinn
   Helpless and cold, I pray,
Amen! I pray, O King,
   To see them pine away.
           Amen!

Bruadar and Smith and Glinn
   May flails of sorrow flay!
Cause for lamenting, snares and cares
   Be theirs by night and day!
           Amen!

Blindness come down on Smith,
   Palsy on Bruadar come,
Amen, O King of Brightness! Smite
   Glinn in his members numb,
           Amen!

Smith in the pangs of pain,
   Stumbling on Bruadar's path,
King of the Elements, Oh, Amen!
   Let loose on Glinn Thy Wrath.
           Amen!

For Bruadar gape the grave,
  Up-shovel for Smith the mould,
Amen, O King of the Sunday! Leave
  Glinn in the devil's hold.
                    Amen!

Terrors on Bruadar rain,
  And pain upon pain on Glinn,
Amen, O King of the Stars! And Smith
  May the devil be linking him.
                    Amen!

Glinn in a shaking ague,
  Cancer on Bruadar's tongue,
Amen, O King of the Heavens! and Smith
  Forever stricken dumb.
                    Amen!

Thirst but no drink for Glinn,
  Smith in a cloud of grief,
Amen! O King of the Saints; and rout
  Bruadar without relief.
                    Amen!

Smith without child or heir,
  And Bruadar bare of store,
Amen, O King of the Friday! Tear
  For Glinn his black heart's core.
                    Amen!

Bruadar with nerveless limbs,
  Hemp strangling Glinn's last breath,
Amen, O King of the World's Light!
  And Smith in grips with death.
                    Amen!

Glinn stiffening for the tomb,
  Smith wasting to decay,
Amen, O King of the Thunder's gloom,
  And Bruadar sick alway.
                    Amen!

Smith like a sieve of holes,
  Bruadar with throat decay,
Amen, O King of the Orders! Glinn
  A buck-show every day.
                Amen!

Hell-hounds to hunt for Smith,
  Glinn led to hang on high,
Amen, O King of the Judgment Day!
  And Bruadar rotting by.
                Amen!

Curses on Glinn, I cry,
  My curse on Bruadar be,
Amen, O King of the Heavens high!
  Let Smith in bondage be.
                Amen!

Showers of want and blame,
  Reproach, and shame of face,
Smite them all three, and smite again,
  Amen, O King of Grace!
                Amen!

Melt, may the three, away,
  Bruadar and Smith and Glinn,
Fall in a swift and sure decay
  And lose, but never win.
                Amen!

May pangs pass through thee, Smith,
  (Let the wind not take my prayer),
May I see before the year is out
  Thy heart's blood flowing there.
                Amen!

Leave Smith no place nor land,
  Let Bruadar wander wide,
May the Devil stand at Glinn's right hand,
  And Glinn to him be tied.
                Amen!

All ill from every airt
  Come down upon the three,
And blast them ere the year be out
  In rout and misery.
            Amen!

Glinn let misfortune bruise,
  Bruadar lose blood and brains,
Amen, O Jesus! hear my voice,
  Let Smith be bent in chains.
            Amen!

I accuse both Glinn and Bruadar,
  And Smith I accuse to God,
May a breach and a gap be upon the three,
  And the Lord's avenging rod.
            Amen!

Each one of the wicked three
  Who raised against me their hand,
May fire from heaven come down and slay
  This day their perjured band,
            Amen!

May none of their race survive,
  May God destroy them all,
Each curse of the psalms in the holy books
  Of the prophets upon them fall.
            Amen!

Blight skull, and ear, and skin,
  And hearing, and voice, and sight,
Amen! before the year be out,
  Blight, Son of the Virgin, blight.
            Amen!

May my curses hot and red
  And all I have said this day,
Strike the Black Peeler, too,
  Amen, dear God, I pray!
            Amen!
      Translated by Douglas Hyde

The Gambler's Repentance

BY LOSS in play men oft forget
   The duty they do owe
To Him that did bestow the same,
   And thousand millions mo.
I loathe to see them swear and stare,
   When they the main have lost;
Forgetting all the byes that were
   With God and Holy Ghost.
By "wounds" and "nails" they think to win,
   But truly it is not so:
For all their frets and fumes in sin
   They moneyless must go.
There is no wight that used it more
   Than he that wrote this verse;
Who crieth Peccavi, now therefore
   His oaths his heart doth pierce.
Therefore example take by me,
   That curse the luckless time
That ever dice mine eyes did see,
   Which bred in me this crime.
Pardon me for that is past,
   I will offend no more,
In this most vile and sinful cast
   Which I will still abhor.

                GERALD, BARON OF OFFALY.

A Curse on a Closed Gate

BE THIS the fate
    Of the man who would shut his gate
On the stranger, gentle or simple, early or late.

When his mouth with a day's long hunger and thirst would
    wish
For the savour of salted fish,
Let him sit and eat his fill of an empty dish.

To the man of that ilk,
Let water stand in his churn, instead of milk
That turns a calf's coat silk.

And under the gloomy night
May never a thatch made tight
Shut out the clouds from his sight.

Above the ground or below it,
Good cheer, may he never know it,
Nor a tale by the fire, nor a dance on the road, nor a song by a
    wandering poet.

Till he open his gate
To the stranger, early or late,
And turn back the stone of his fate.

JAMES H. COUSINS
From the Irish.

O'Hussey's Ode to the Maguire

WHERE is my chief, my master, this bleak night, mavrone?
  O cold, cold, miserably cold is this bleak night for Hugh!
Its showery, arrowy, speary sleet pierceth one thro' and thro',
Pierceth one to the very bone.

Rolls real thunder? Or was that red vivid light
Only a meteor? I scarce know; but through the midnight
    dim
The pitiless ice-wind streams. Except the hate that perse-
    cutes him,
Nothing hath crueler venomy might.

An awful, a tremendous night is this, meseems!
The flood-gates of the rivers of heaven, I think, have been
    burst wide;
Down from the overcharged clouds, like to headlong ocean's
    tide,
Descends grey rain in roaring streams.

Tho' he were even a wolf ranging the round green woods,
Tho' he were even a pleasant salmon in the unchainable sea,
Tho' he were a wild mountain eagle, he could scarce bear, he,
This sharp sore sleet, these howling floods.

O mournful is my soul this night for Hugh Maguire!
Darkly as in a dream he strays. Before him and behind
Triumphs the tyrannous anger of the wounding wind,
The wounding wind that burns as fire.

It is my bitter grief, it cuts me to the heart
That in the country of Clan Darry this should be his fate!
O woe is me, where is he? Wandering, houseless, desolate,
Alone, without or guide or chart!

Medreams I see just now his face, the strawberry-bright,
Uplifted to the blackened heavens, while the tempestuous
    winds
Blow fiercely over and round him, and the smiting sleet-
    shower blinds
The hero of Galang to-night!

Large, large affliction unto me and mine it is
That one of his majestic bearing, his fair stately form,
Should thus be tortured and o'erborne; that this unsparing
    storm
Should wreak its wrath on head like his!

That his great hand, so oft the avenger of the oppressed,
Should this chill churlish night, perchance, be paralysed by
    frost;
While through some icicle-hung thicket, as one lorn and lost,
He walks and wanders without rest.

The tempest-driven torrent deluges the mead,
It overflows the low banks of the rivulets and ponds;
The lawns and pasture-grounds lie locked in icy bonds,
So that the cattle cannot feed.

The pale-bright margins of the streams are seen by none;
Rushes and sweeps along the untamable flood on every side;
It penetrates and fills the cottagers' dwellings far and wide;
Water and land are blent in one.

Through some dark woods, 'mid bones of monsters, Hugh
    now strays,
As he confronts the storm with anguished heart, but manly
    brow,
O what a sword-wound to that tender heart of his, were now
A backward glance at peaceful days!

But other thoughts are his, thoughts that can still inspire
With joy and onward-bounding hope the bosom of MacNee;
Thoughts of his warriors charging like bright billows of the
    sea,
Borne on the wind's wings, flashing fire!

And tho' frost glaze to-night the clear dew of his eyes,
And white ice-gauntlets glove his noble fine fair fingers o'er,
A warm dress is to him that lightning-garb he ever wore,
The lightning of his soul, not skies.

Avran.

Hugh marched forth to fight: I grieved to see him so de-
    part.
And lo! to-night he wanders frozen, rain-drenched, sad be-
    trayed;
But the memory of the lime-white mansions his right hand
    hath laid
In ashes, warms the hero's heart!
                Translated by JAMES CLARENCE MANGAN.

A Lament for the Princes of Tyrone and Tyrconnel

O WOMAN of the piercing wail,
　Who mournest o'er yon mound of clay
With sigh and groan,
Would God thou wert among the Gael!
Thou would'st not then from day to day
Weep thus alone.
'Twere long before around a grave
In green Tyrconnel, one could find
This loneliness;
Near where Beann-Boirche's banners wave,
Such grief as thine could ne'er have pined
Companionless.

Beside the wave in Donegal,
In Antrim's glens, or fair Dromore,
Or Killilee,
Or where the sunny waters fall
At Assaroe, near Erna shore,
This could not be.
On Derry's plains, in rich Drumcliff,
Throughout Armagh the Great, renowned
In olden years,
No day could pass but woman's grief
Would rain upon the burial-ground
Fresh floods of tears!

O no!—From Shannon, Boyne, and Suir,
From high Dunluce's castle-walls,
From Lissadill,

Would flock alike both rich and poor:
One wail would rise from Cruachan's halls
To Tara Hill;
And some would come from Barrow-side,
And many a maid would leave her home
On Leitrim's plains,
And by melodious Banna's tide,
And by the Mourne and Erne, to come
And swell thy strains!

O, horses' hoofs would trample down
The mount whereon the martyr-saint
Was crucified;
From glen and hill, from plain and town,
One loud lament, one thrilling plaint,
Would echo wide.
There would not soon be found, I ween,
One foot of ground among those bands
For museful thought,
So many shriekers of the keen
Would cry aloud, and clap their hands,
All woe-distraught!

Two princes of the line of Conn
Sleep in their cells of clay beside
O'Donnell Roe:
Three royal youths, alas! are gone,
Who lived for Erin's weal, but died
For Erin's woe.
Ah, could the men of Ireland read
The names those noteless burial-stones
Display to view,
Their wounded hearts afresh would bleed,
Their tears gush forth again, their groans
Resound anew!

The youths whose relics moulder here
Were sprung from Hugh, high prince and lord
Of Aileach's lands;
Thy noble brothers, justly dear,
Thy nephew, long to be deplored
By Ulster's bands.
Theirs were not souls wherein dull time
Could domicile decay, or house
Decrepitude!
They passed from earth ere manhood's prime,
Ere years had power to dim their brows,
Or chill their blood.

And who can marvel o'er thy grief,
Or who can blame thy flowing tears,
Who knows their source?
O'Donnell, Dunnasava's chief,
Cut off amid his vernal years,
Lies here a corse
Beside his brother Cathbar, whom
Tyrconnell of the Helmets mourns
In deep despair:
For valour, truth, and comely bloom,
For all that greatens and adorns,
A peerless pair.

Oh, had these twain, and he, the third,
The Lord of Mourne, O'Niall's son
(Their mate in death),
A prince in look, in deed, and word,
Had these three heroes yielded on
The field their breath,
Oh, had they fallen on Criffan's plain,
There would not be a town or clan
From shore to sea,
But would with shrieks bewail the slain,
Or chant aloud the exulting rann
Of jubilee!

When high the shout of battle rose,
On fields where Freedom's torch still burned
Through Erin's gloom,
If one, if barely one of those
Were slain, all Ulster would have mourned
The hero's doom!
If at Athboy, where hosts of brave
Ulidian horsemen sank beneath
The shock of spears,
Young Hugh O'Neill had found a grave,
Long must the North have wept his death
With heart-wrung tears!

If on the day of Ballach-myre
The Lord of Mourne had met thus young,
A warrior's fate,
In vain would such as thou desire
To mourn, alone, the champion sprung
From Niall the Great!
No marvel this—for all the dead,
Heaped on the field, pile over pile,
At Mullach-brack,
Were scarce an eric for his head,
If death had stayed his footsteps while
On victory's track!

If on the Day of Hostages
The fruit had from the parent bough
Been rudely torn
In sight of Munster's bands—MacNee's—
Such blow the blood of Conn, I trow,
Could ill have borne.
If on the day of Ballach-boy
Some arm had laid by foul surprise,
The chieftain low,
Even our victorious shout of joy
Would soon give place to rueful cries
And groans of woe!

If on the day the Saxon host
Were forced to fly—a day so great
For Ashanee—
The Chief had been untimely lost,
Our conquering troops should moderate
Their mirthful glee.
There would not lack on Lifford's day,
From Galway, from the glens of Boyle,
From Limerick's towers,
A marshalled file, a long array
Of mourners to bedew the soil
With tears in showers!

If on the day a sterner fate
Compelled his flight from Athenree,
His blood had flowed,
What numbers all disconsolate,
Would come unasked, and share with thee
Affliction's load!
If Derry's crimson field had seen
His life-blood offered up, though 'twere
On Victory's shrine,
A thousand cries would swell the keen,
A thousand voices of despair
Would echo thine!

Oh, had the fierce Dalcassian swarm
That bloody night of Fergus' banks
But slain our Chief,
When rose his camp in wild alarm—
How would the triumph of his ranks
Be dashed with grief!
How would the troops of Murbach mourn
If on the Curlew Mountains' day
Which England rued,
Some Saxon hand had left them lorn,
By shedding there, amid the fray,
Their prince's blood!

Red would have been our warriors' eyes
Had Roderick found on Sligo's field
A gory grave,
No Northern Chief would soon arise
So sage to guide, so strong to shield,
So swift to save.
Long would Leith-Cuinn have wept if Hugh
Had met the death he oft had dealt
Among the foe;
But, had our Roderick fallen too,
All Erin must, alas! have felt
The deadly blow!

What do I say? Ah, woe is me!
Already we bewail in vain
Their fatal fall!
And Erin, once the great and free,
Now vainly mourns her breakless chain,
And iron thrall.
Then, daughter of O'Donnell, dry
Thine overflowing eyes, and turn
Thy heart aside,
For Adam's race is born to die,
And sternly the sepulchral urn
Mocks human pride.

Look not, nor sigh, for earthly throne,
Nor place thy trust in arm of clay,
But on thy knees
Uplift thy soul to God alone,
For all things go their destined way
As He decrees.
Embrace the faithful crucifix,
And seek the path of pain and prayer
Thy Saviour trod;
Nor let thy spirit intermix
With earthly hope, with worldly care,
Its groans to God!

And Thou, O mighty Lord! whose ways
Are far above our feeble minds
To understand,
Sustain us in these doleful days,
And render light the chain that binds
Our fallen land!

JAMES CLARENCE MANGAN: *Translated from the Irish.*

Lament for the Death of Eoghan Ruadh O'Neill

"DID they dare, did they dare, to slay Eoghan Ruadh
O'Neill?"
"Yes, they slew with poison him they feared to meet with
steel."
"May God wither up their hearts! May their blood cease
to flow,
May they walk in living death, who poisoned Eoghan Ruadh."

"Though it break my heart to hear, say again the bitter
words.
From Derry, against Cromwell, he marched to measure
swords:
But the weapon of the Sassanach met him on his way.
And he died at Cloch Uachtar, upon St. Leonard's day.

"Wail, wail ye for the Mighty One. Wail, wail ye for the
Dead,
Quench the hearth, and hold the breath—with ashes strew the
head.
How tenderly we loved him. How deeply we deplore!
Holy Saviour! but to think we shall never see him more!

"Sagest in the council was he, kindest in the hall,
Sure we never won a battle—'twas Eoghan won them all.
Had he lived—had he lived—our dear country had been free:
But he's dead, but he's dead, and 'tis slaves we'll ever be.

"O'Farrell and Clanricarde, Preston and Red Hugh,
Audley and MacMahon—ye are valiant, wise and true:
But—what are ye all to our darling who is gone?
The Rudder of our Ship was he, our Castle's corner stone.

"Wail, wail him through the Island! Weep, weep for our
    pride!
Would that on the battlefield our gallant chief had died!
Weep the Victor of Beinn Burb—weep him, young and old:
Weep for him, ye women—your beautiful lies cold!

"We thought you would not die—we were sure you would
    not go,
And leave us in our utmost need to Cromwell's cruel blow—
Sheep without a shepherd, when the snow shuts out the
    sky—
O! why did you leave us, Eoghan? Why did you die?

"Soft as woman's was your voice, O'Neill! bright was your
    eye,
O! why did you leave us, Eoghan? Why did you die?
Your troubles are all over, you're at rest with God on high,
But we're slaves, and we're orphans, Eoghan!—why did you
    die?"

THOMAS DAVIS.

Dirge on the Death of Art O'Leary

By Dark Eileen, his wife

I

MY CLOSEST and dearest!
　From the first day I saw you
From the top of the market-house,
My eyes gave heed to you,
My heart gave affection to you,
I fled from my friends with you,
Far from my home with you,
No lasting sorrow this to me.

II

Thou didst bring me to fair chambers,
Rooms you had adorned for me;
Ovens were reddened for me,
Fresh trout were caught for me,
Roast flesh was carved for me
From beef that was felled for me;
On beds of down I lay
Till the coming of the milking-time,
Or so long as was pleasing to me.

225

Rider of the white palm!
With the silver-hilted sword!
Well your beaver hat became you
With its band of graceful gold;
Your suit of solid homespun yarn
Wrapped close around your form;
Slender shoes of foreign fashion,
And a pin of brightest silver
Fastened in your shirt.
As you rode in stately wise
On your slender steed, white-faced,
After coming over seas,
Even the Saxons bowed before you
Bowed down to the very ground;
Not because they loved you well
But from deadly hate;
For it was by them you fell,
Darling of my soul.

My friend and my little calf!
Offsprings of the Lords of Antrim,
And the chiefs of Immokely!
Never had I thought you dead,
Until there came to me your mare
Her bridle dragged beside her to the ground;
Upon her brow your heart-blood splashed,
Even to the carven saddle flowing down
Where you were wont to sit or stand.
I did not stay to cleanse it—
I gave a quick leap with my hands
Upon the wooden stretcher of the bed;
A second leap was to the gate,
And the third leap upon thy mare.

V

In haste I clapped my hands together,
I followed on your tracks
As well as I could,
Till I found you laid before me dead
At the foot of a lowly bush of furze;
Without pope, without bishop,
Without cleric or priest
To read a psalm for thee;
But only an old bent wasted crone
Who flung over thee the corner of her cloak.

My dear and beloved one!
When it will come to me to reach our home,
Little Conor, of our love,
And Fiac, his toddling baby-brother,
Will be asking of me quickly
Where I left their dearest father?
I shall answer them with sorrow
That I left him in Kill Martyr;
They will call upon their father;
He will not be there to answer.

My love and my chosen one!
When you were going forward from the gate,
You turned quickly back again!
You kissed your two children,
You threw a kiss to me.
You said, "Eileen, arise now, be stirring,
And set your house in order,
Be swiftly moving.
I am leaving our home,
It is likely that I may not come again."
I took it only for a jest
You used often to be jesting thus before.

My friend and my heart's love!
Arise up, my Art,
Leap on thy steed,
Arise out to Macroom
And to Inchegeela after that;
A bottle of wine in thy grasp,
As was ever in the time of thy ancestors.
Arise up, my Art,
Rider of the shining sword;
Put on your garments,
Your fair noble clothes;
Don your black beaver,
Draw on your gloves;
See, here hangs your whip,
Your good mare waits without;
Strike eastward on the narrow road,
For the bushes will bare themselves before you,
For the streams will narrow on your path,
For men and women will bow themselves before you
If their own good manners are upon them yet,
But I am much a-feared they are not now.

Destruction to you and woe,
O Morris, hideous the treachery
That took from me the man of the house,
The father of my babes;
Two of them running about the house,
The third beneath my breast,
It is likely that I shall not give it birth.

My long wound, my bitter sorrow,
That I was not beside thee
When the shot was fired;
That I might have got it in my soft body
Or in the skirt of my gown;
Till I would give you freedom to escape,
O Rider of the grey eye,
Because it is you would best have followed after
    them.

My dear and my heart's love!
Terrible to me the way I see thee,
To be putting our hero,
Our rider so true of heart,
In a little cap in a coffin!
Thou who used to be fishing along the streams,
Thou who didst drink within wide halls
Among the gentle women white of breast;
It is my thousand afflictions
That I have lost your companionship!
My love and my darling,
Could my shouts but reach thee
West in mighty Derrynane,
And in Carhen of the yellow apples after that;
Many a light-hearted young horseman,
And woman with white, spotless kerchief
Would swiftly be with us here,
To wail above thy head
Art O'Leary of the joyous laugh!
O women of the soft, wet eyes,
Stay now your weeping,
Till Art O'Leary drinks his drink
Before his going back to school;
Not to learn reading or music does he go there now,
But to carry clay and stones.

XII

My love and my secret thou.
Thy corn-stacks are piled,
And thy golden kine are milking,
But it is upon my own heart is the grief!
There is no healing in the Province of Munster,
Nor in the Island smithy of the Fians,
Till Art O'Leary will come back to me;
But all as if it were a lock upon a trunk
And the key of it gone straying;
Or till rust will come upon the screw.

XIII

My friend and my best one!
Art O'Leary, son of Conor,
Son of Cadach, son of Lewis,
Eastward from wet wooded glens,
Westward from the slender hill
Where the rowan-berries grow,
And the yellow nuts are ripe upon the branches;
Apples trailing, as it was in my day.
Little wonder to myself
If fires were lighted in O'Leary's country,
And at the mouth of Ballingeary,
Or at holy Gougane Barra of the cells,
After the rider of the smooth grip,
After the huntsman unwearied
When, heavy breathing with the chase,
Even thy lithe deerhounds lagged behind.
O horseman of the enticing eyes,
What happened thee last night?
For I myself thought
That the whole world could not kill you
When I bought for you that shirt of mail.

XIV

My friend and my darling!
A cloudy vision through the darkness
Came to me last night,
At Cork lately
And I alone upon my bed!
I saw the wooded glen withered,
I saw our lime-washed court fallen;
No sound of speech came from thy hunting-dogs
Nor sound of singing from the birds
When you were found in the clay,
On the side of the hill without;
When you were found fallen
Art O'Leary;
With your drop of blood oozing out
Through the breast of your shirt.

XV

It is known to Jesus Christ,
I will put no cap upon thy head,
Nor body-linen on my side,
Nor shoes upon my feet,
Nor gear throughout the house:
Even on the brown mare will be no bridle,
But I shall spend all in taking the law.
I will go across the seas
To seek the villain of the black blood
But if they will give no heed to me,
It is I that will come back again
To speak with the King;
Who cut off my treasure from me.
O Morris, who killed my hero,
Was there not one man in Erin
Would put a bullet through you?

XVI

The affection of this heart to you,
O white women of the mill,
For the edged poetry that you have shed
Over the horseman of the brown mare.
It is I who am the lonely one
In Inse Carriganane.

Translated by ELEANOR HULL.

The Lament for O'Sullivan Beare
(*Made by His Nurse*)

THE sun of Ivera
  No longer shines brightly,
The voice of her music
No longer is sprightly;
No more to her maidens
The light dance is dear,
Since the death of our darling
O'Sullivan Beare.

Scully! thou false one
You basely betrayed him;
In his strong hour of need
When thy right hand should aid him;
He fed thee—he clad thee—
You had all could delight thee:
You left him, you sold him
May heaven requite thee!

Scully! May all kinds
Of evil attend thee!
On thy dark road of life
May no kind one befriend thee!
May fevers long burn thee,
And agues long freeze thee!
May the strong hand of God
In his red anger seize thee!

Had he died calmly
I would not deplore him;
Or if the wild strife
Of the sea-war closed o'er him:
But with ropes round his white limbs
Through Ocean to trail him,
Like a fish after slaughter
'Tis therefore I wail him.

Long may the curse
Of his people pursue them;
Scully that sold him
And soldier that slew him!
One glimpse of Heaven's light
May they see never!
May the hearthstone of Hell
Be their best bed forever!

In the hole where the vile hands
Of soldiers had laid thee,
Unhonored, unshrouded,
And headless they laid thee,
No eye to rain o'er thee,
No dirge to lament thee,
No friend to deplore thee!

Dear head of my darling
How gory and pale
These aged eyes see thee,
High spiked on their jail!
That cheek in the summer sun
Ne'er shall grow warm;
Nor that eye e'er catch light
From the flash of the storm!

A curse, blessed ocean,
Is on thy green water
From the Haven of Cork
To Ivera of slaughter:
Since the billows were dyed
With the red wounds of fear
Of Muirtach Og
Our O'Sullivan Beare!
Translated by JEREMIAH JOSEPH CALLANAN.

A Connacht Caoine

DRAW near to the tables, ye that wear the cloaks;
  Here ye have flesh, but it is not roast flesh,
Nor boiled in pots, nor cooked for feasting,
But my dear Bourke—och, och, after been slain.

You, young women, who are drinking wine there,
Let my sharp screeches pierce your heart.
If I am wise I may get whatever is my lot,
But you will never—och, och, och—get another brother!

O young woman, don't you pity my sorrow?
My mourning over the bier of my spouse?
A lock of his hair is within my purse,
And his offspring—och, och—hidden within me!

From the Irish.

The Convict of Clonmala

HOW hard is my fortune,
  And vain my repining!
The strong rope of fate
For this young neck is twining.
My strength is departed,
My cheek sunk and sallow,
While I languish in chains
In the gaol of Clonmala.

No boy in the village
Was ever yet milder;
I'd play with a child
And my sport would be wilder;
I'd dance without tiring
From morning till even,
And the goal-ball I'd strike
To the lightning of heaven.

At my bed-foot decaying,
My hurl-ball is lying;
Through the boys of the village
My goal-ball is flying;
My horse 'mong the neighbors
Neglected may fallow,
While I pine in my chains
In the gaol of Clonmala.

Next Sunday the pattern
At home will be keeping,
And the young active hurlers
The field will be sweeping;
With the dance of fair maidens
The evening they'll hallow,
While this heart, once so gay,
Shall be cold in Clonmala.

Translated by JEREMIAH JOSEPH CALLANAN.

The Outlaw of Loch Lene

OH, many a day have I made good ale in the glen,
That came not from stream, or malt, like the brewing of
men;
My bed was the ground; my roof, the greenwood above,
And all the wealth that I sought, one fair kind glance from my
love.

Alas! On the night when the horses I drove from the field,
That I was not near, from terror my angel to shield!
She stretched forth her arms, her mantle she flung on the wind,
And swam o'er Loch Lene, her outlawed lover to find.

Oh, would that a freezing, sleet-winged tempest did sweep,
And I and my love were alone far off on the deep!
I'd ask not a ship, or a bark, or a pinnace to save—
With her arm round my waist, I'd fear not the wind nor the wave.

'Tis down by the lake where the wild tree fringes its sides,
That the maid of my heart, the fair one of heaven resides:
I think, as at eve she wanders its mazes along,
The birds go to sleep by the sweet wild twist of her song.

From the Irish: JEREMIAH JOSEPH CALLANAN.

Aghadoe

THERE'S a glade in Aghadoe, Aghadoe, Aghadoe,
 There's a green and silent glade in Aghadoe,
  Where we met, my Love and I, Love's fair planet in the
   sky,
O'er that sweet and silent glade in Aghadoe.

There's a glen in Aghadoe, Aghadoe, Aghadoe,
There's a deep and secret glen in Aghadoe,
  Where I hid him from the eyes of the red-coats and their
   spies
That year the trouble came to Aghadoe.

Oh! my curse on one black heart in Aghadoe, Aghadoe,
On Shaun Dhuv, my mother's son in Aghadoe,
  When your throat fries in hell's drouth salt the flame be in
   your mouth,
For the treachery you did in Aghadoe!

For they tracked me to that glen in Aghadoe, Aghadoe,
When the price was on his head in Aghadoe;
  O'er the mountain through the wood, as I stole to him
   with food,
When in hiding lone he lay in Aghadoe.

But they never took him living in Aghadoe, Aghadoe;
With the bullets in his heart in Aghadoe,
  There he lay, the head—my breast keeps the warmth where
   once 'twould rest—
Gone, to win the traitor's gold from Aghadoe!

I walked to Mallow Town from Aghadoe, Aghadoe,
Brought his head from the gaol's gate to Aghadoe,

Then I covered him with fern, and I piled on him the
    cairn,
Like an Irish king he sleeps in Aghadoe.

Oh, to creep into that cairn in Aghadoe, Aghadoe!
There to rest upon his breast in Aghadoe!
    Sure your dog for you could die with no truer heart than
    I—
Your own love cold on your cairn in Aghadoe.

JOHN TODHUNTER.

The Burial of Sir John Moore

NOT a drum was heard, not a funeral note,
  As his corse to the rampart we hurried;
Not a soldier discharged his farewell shot
  O'er the grave where our hero we buried.

We buried him darkly at dead of night,
  The sods with our bayonets turning,
By the struggling moonbeam's misty light,
  And the lantern dimly burning.

No useless coffin enclosed his breast,
  Not in sheet or in shroud we wound him;
But he lay like a warrior taking his rest,
  With his martial cloak around him.

Few and short were the prayers we said,
  And we spoke not a word of sorrow;
But we steadfastly gazed on the face that was dead,
  And we bitterly thought of the morrow

We thought as we hollow'd his narrow bed,
  And smooth'd down his lonely pillow,
That the foe and the stranger would tread o'er his
    head,
  And we far away on the billow!

Lightly they'll talk of the spirit that's gone,
  And o'er his cold ashes upbraid him,
But little he'll reck, if they let him sleep on
  In the grave where a Briton has laid him.

But half of our heavy task was done,
  When the clock struck the hour for retiring;
And we heard the distant and random gun
  That the foe was sullenly firing.

Slowly and sadly we laid him down,
  From the field of his fame fresh and gory;
We carved not a line, and we raised not a stone—
  But we left him alone in his glory!

                              CHARLES WOLFE.

Lament for Thomas Davis

I WALKED through Ballinderry in the spring-time,
  When the bud was on the tree;
And I said, in every fresh-ploughed field beholding
  The sowers striding free,
Scattering broadside forth the corn in golden plenty
  On the quick seed-clasping soil,
"Even such this day, among the fresh-stirred hearts of Erin,
Thomas Davis, is thy toil."

I sat by Ballyshannon in the summer,
  And saw the salmon leap;
And I said, as I beheld the gallant creatures
  Spring glittering from the deep,
Through the spray, and through the prone heaps striving
      onward
  To the calm, clear streams above,
"So seekest thou thy native founts of freedom, Thomas
      Davis,
  In thy brightness of strength and love."

I stood in Derrybawn in the autumn,
  And I heard the eagle call,
With a clangorous cry of wrath and lamentation
  That filled the wide mountain hall,
O'er the bare, deserted place of his plundered eyrie;
  And I said, as he screamed and soared,
"So callest thou, thou wrathful, soaring Thomas Davis,
  For a nation's rights restored!"

And, alas! to think but now, and thou art lying,
  Dear Davis, dead at thy mother's knee;
And I, no mother near, on my own sick-bed,
  That face on earth shall never see;
I may lie and try to feel that I am dreaming,
  I may lie and try to say, "Thy will be done,"
But a hundred such as I will never comfort Erin
  For the loss of the noble son!

Young husbandman of Erin's fruitful seed-time,
  In the fresh track of danger's plough!
Who will walk the heavy, toilsome, perilous furrow,
  Girt with freedom's seed-sheets, now?
Who will banish with the wholesome crop of knowledge
  The daunting weed and the bitter thorn,
Now that thou thyself art but a seed for hopeful planting
  Against the Resurrection morn?

Young salmon of the flood-tide of freedom
  That swells round Erin's shore!
Thou wilt leap against their loud oppressive torrent
  Of bigotry and hate no more;
Drawn downward by their prone material instinct,
  Let them thunder on their rocks and foam—
Thou hast leapt, aspiring soul, to founts beyond their raging,
  Where troubled waters never come!

But I grieve not, Eagle of the empty eyrie,
  That thy wrathful cry is still;
And that the songs alone of peaceful mourners
  Are heard to-day on Earth's hill;
Better far, if brothers' war be destined for us
  (God avert that horrid day I pray),
That ere our hands be stained with slaughter fratricidal,
  Thy warm heart should be cold in clay.

245

But my trust is strong in God, Who made us brothers,
  That He will not suffer their right hands,
Which thou hast joined in holier rites than wedlock
  To draw opposing brands.
Oh, many a tuneful tongue that thou madest vocal
  Would lie cold and silent then;
And songless long once more, should often-widowed Erin
  Mourn the loss of her brave young men.

Oh, brave young men, my love, my pride, my promise,
  'Tis on you my hopes are set,
In manliness, in kindliness, in justice,
  To make Erin a nation yet;
Self-respecting, self-relying, self-advancing—
  In union or in severance, free and strong—
And if God grant this, then, under God, to Thomas Davis
  Let the greater praise belong.
                              SIR SAMUEL FERGUSON.

Parnell

TEARS will betray all pride, but when ye mourn him,
    Be it in soldier wise;
As for a captain who hath greatly borne him,
    And in the midnight dies.

Fewness of words is best; he was too great
    For ours or any phrase.
Love could not guess, nor the slipped hound of hate
    Track his soul's secret ways.

Signed with a sign, unbroken, unrevealed,
    His Calvary he trod;
So let him keep, where all world-wounds are healed
    The silences of God.

Yet is he Ireland's, too: a flaming coal
    Lit at the stars, and sent
To burn the sin of patience from her soul
    The scandal of content.

A name to be a trumpet of attack;
    And, in the evil stress,
For England's iron No! to fling her back
    A grim, granatic Yes.

He taught us more, this best as it was last:
    When comrades go apart
They shall go greatly, cancelling the past,
    Slaying the kindlier heart.

Friendship and love, all clean things and unclean,
　Shall be as drifted leaves,
Spurned by our Ireland's feet, that queenliest Queen
　Who gives not, but receives.

So freedom comes, and comes no other wise;
　He gave—"The Chief" gave well;
Limned in his blood across your clearing skies
　Look up and read: Parnell!

THOMAS KETTLE.

248

Synge's Grave

MY grief! that they have laid you in the town
Within the moidher of its thousand wheels
And busy feet that travel up and down.

They had a right to choose a better bed
Far off among the hills where silence steals
In on the soul with comfort-bringing tread.

The curlew would have keened for you all day,
The wind across the heather cried Ochone
For sorrow of his brother gone away.

In Glenmalure, far off from town-bred men,
Why would they not have left your sleep alone
At peace there in the shadow of the glen?

To tend your grave you should have had the sun,
The fraughan and the moss, the heather brown
And gorse turned gold for joy of Spring begun.

You should have had your brothers, wind and rain,
And in the dark the stars all looking down
To ask, "When will he take the road again?"

The herdsmen of the lone back hills, that drive
The mountain ewes to some far distant fair,
Would stand and say, "We knew him well alive,

That God may rest his soul!" then they would pass
Into the silence brooding everywhere,
And leave you to your sleep below the grass.

But now among these alien city graves,
What way are you without the rough wind's breath
You free-born son of mountains and wild waves?

Ah! God knows better—here you've no abode,
So long ago you had the laugh at death,
And rose and took the windswept mountain road.
                                    WINIFRED LETTS.

Revelry for the Dying

WE MEET 'neath the sounding rafter
   And the walls around are bare;
As they shout to our peals of laughter,
It seems that the dead are there.
But stand to your glasses—steady!
We drink to our comrades' eyes;
Quaff a cup to the dead already,
And hurrah for the next that dies!

Not here are the goblets glowing,
Not here is the vintage sweet;
'Tis cold as our hearts are growing,
And dark as the doom we meet.
But stand to your glasses—steady!
And soon shall our pulses rise;
A cup to the dead already,
And hurrah for the next that dies!

Not a sigh for the lot that darkles,
Not a tear for the friends that sink,
We'll fall mid the wine-cup's sparkles,
As mute as the wine we drink.
So stand to your glasses—steady!
'Tis this that the respite buys;
One cup to the dead already,
And hurrah for the next that dies!

Time was when we frowned on others;
We thought we were wiser then.
Ha! Ha! let those think of their mothers
Who hopes to see them again.
No! stand to your glasses—steady!
The thoughtless are here the wise;
A cup to the dead already,
And hurrah for the next that dies!

There's many a hand that's shaking,
There's many a cheek that's sunk;
But soon, though our hearts are breaking,
They'll burn with the wine we've drunk.
So stand to your glasses—steady!
'Tis here the revival lies;
A cup to the dead already,
And hurrah for the next that dies!

There's a mist on the glass congealing,
'Tis the hurricane's fiery breath;
And thus does the warmth of feeling
Turn ice in the grasp of death;
Ho! stand to your glasses—steady!
For a moment the vapor flies;
A cup for the dead already,
And hurrah for the next that dies!

Who dreads to the dust returning?
Who shrinks from the sable shore,
Where the high and haughty yearning
Of the soul shall sting no more?
Ho! stand to your glasses—steady!
The world is a world of lies;
A cup to the dead already,
And hurrah for the next that dies!

Cast off from the land that bore us,
Betrayed by the land we find,
Where the brightest have gone before us,
And the dullest remain behind—
Stand, stand to your glasses—steady!
'Tis all we have left to prize;
A cup to the dead already,
And hurrah for the next that dies!

BARTHOLOMEW DOWLING.

Lament for Sean MacDermott

THEY have slain you, Sean MacDermott; never more these
    eyes will greet
The eyes beloved by women, and the smile that true men
    loved;
Never more I'll hear the stick-tap, and the gay and limping
    feet,
They have slain you, Sean the gentle, Sean the valiant, Sean
    the proved.

Have you scorn for us who linger here behind you, Sean the
    wise?
As you look about and greet your comrades in the strange
    new dawn.
So one says, but saying, wrongs you, for doubt never dimmed
    your eyes,
And not death itself could make those lips of yours grow
    bitter, Sean.

As your stick goes tapping down the heavenly pavement,
    Sean, my friend,
That is not your way of thinking, generous, tender, wise and
    brave;
We, who knew and loved and trusted you, are trusted to the
    end,
And your hand even now grips mine as though there never
    were a grave.

SEUMAS O'SULLIVAN.

Lament for Thomas MacDonagh

HE SHALL not hear the bittern cry
  In the wild sky, where he is lain,
Nor voices of the sweeter birds
Above the wailing of the rain.

Nor shall he know when loud March blows
Thro' slanting snows her fanfare shrill,
Blowing to flame the golden cup
Of many an upset daffodil.

But when the Dark Cow leaves the moor,
And pastures poor with greedy weeds,
Perhaps he'll hear her low at morn,
Lifting her horn in pleasant meads.

FRANCIS LEDWIDGE.

Lament for the Poets: 1916

I HEARD the Poor Old Woman say:
"At break of day the fowler came,
And took my blackbirds from their songs
Who loved me well thro' shame and blame.

No more from lovely distances
Their songs shall bless me mile by mile,
Nor to white Ashbourne call me down
To wear my crown another while.

With bended flowers the angels mark
For the skylark the place they lie,
From there its little family
Shall dip their wings first in the sky.

And when the first surprise of flight
Sweet songs excite, from the far dawn
Shall there come blackbirds loud with love,
Sweet echoes of the singers gone.

But in the lonely hush of eve
Weeping I grieve the silent bills."
I heard the Poor Old Woman say
In Derry of the little hills.

FRANCIS LEDWIDGE.

How Oft Has the Banshee Cried

HOW oft has the Banshee cried!
　How oft has death untied
Bright links that Glory wove,
Sweet bonds entwined by Love!
Peace to each manly soul that sleepeth;
Rest to each faithful eye that weepeth;
　Long may the fair and brave
　Sigh o'er the hero's grave!

　We're fallen on evil days!
　Star after star decays,
　Every bright name that shed
　Light o'er the land is fled.
Dark falls the tear of him that mourneth
Lost joy, or hope that ne'er returneth:
　But brightly flows the tear
　Wept o'er a hero's bier.

　Quenched are our beacon lights—
　Thou, of the Hundred Fights!
　Thou, on whose burning tongue
　Truth, peace and freedom hung!
Both mute—but long as valor shineth,
Or mercy's soul at war repineth,
　So long shall Erin's pride
　Tell how they lived and died.
　　　　　　　　THOMAS MOORE.

PART VI
OUR HERITAGE

The Downfall of the Gael

MY HEART is in woe,
   And my soul deep in trouble,—
For the mighty are low,
And abased are the noble:

The Sons of the Gael
Are in exile and mourning,
Worn, weary, and pale
As spent pilgrims returning;

Or men who, in flight
From the field of disaster,
Beseech the black night
On their flight to fall faster;

Or seamen aghast
When their planks gape asunder,
And the waves fierce and fast
Tumble through in hoarse thunder;

Or men whom we see
That have got their death-omen,—
Such wretches are we
In the chains of our foemen!

Our courage is fear,
Our nobility vileness,
Our hope is despair,
And our comeliness foulness.

There is mist on our heads,
And a cloud chill and hoary
Of black sorrow, sheds
An eclipse on our glory.

From Boyne to the Linn
Has the mandate been given,
That the children of Finn
From their country be driven.

That the sons of the king—
Oh, the treason and malice!—
Shall no more ride the ring
In their own native valleys;

No more shall repair
Where the hill foxes tarry,
Nor forth to the air
Fling the hawk at her quarry:

For the plain shall be broke
By the share of the stranger,
And the stone-mason's stroke
Tell the woods of their danger;

The green hills and shore
Be with white keeps disfigured,
And the Mote of Rathmore
Be the Saxon churl's haggard!

The land of the lakes
Shall no more know the prospect
Of valleys and brakes—
So transformed is her aspect!

The Gael cannot tell,
In the uprooted wildwood
And the red ridgy dell,
The old nurse of his childhood:

The nurse of his youth
Is in doubt as she views him,
If the wan wretch, in truth,
Be the child of her bosom.

We starve by the board,
And we thirst amid wassail—
For the guest is the lord,
And the host is the vassal!

Through the woods let us roam,
Through the wastes wild and barren;
We are strangers at home!
We are exiles in Erin!

And Erin's a bark
O'er the wide waters driven!
And the tempest howls dark,
And her side planks are riven!

And in billows of might
Swell the Saxon before her,—
Unite, oh, unite!
Or the billows burst o'er her!
Translated by SIR SAMUEL FERGUSON.

Lament for Banba

O MY land! O my love!
    What a woe, and how deep,
Is thy death to my long mourning soul!
    God alone, God above,
    Can awake thee from sleep,
Can release thee from bondage and dole!
    Alas, alas, and alas!
        For the once proud people of Banba!

As a tree in its prime,
    Which the axe layeth low,
Didst thou fall, O unfortunate land!
    Not by time, nor thy crime,
    Came the shock and the blow.
They were given by a false felon hand!
    Alas, alas, and alas!
        For the once proud people of Banba!

O, my grief of all griefs
    Is to see how thy throne
Is usurped, whilst thyself art in thrall!
    Other lands have their chiefs,
    Have their kings, thou alone
Art a wife, yet a widow withal!
    Alas, alas, and alas!
        For the once proud people of Banba!

The high house of O'Neill
    Is gone down to the dust,
The O'Brien is clanless and banned;
    And the steel, the red steel
    May no more be the trust
Of the Faithful and Brave in the land!
    Alas, alas, and alas!
        For the once proud people of Banba!

True, alas! Wrong and Wrath
    Were of old all too rife.
Deeds were done which no good man admires
    And perchance Heaven hath
    Chastened us for the strife
And the blood-shedding ways of our sires!
    Alas, alas, and alas!
        For the once proud people of Banba!

But, no more! This our doom,
    While our hearts yet are warm,
Let us not over weakly deplore!
    For the hour soon may loom
    When the Lord's mighty hand
Shall be raised for our rescue once more!
    And all our grief shall be turned into joy
        For the still proud people of Banba!
Translated by JAMES CLARENCE MANGAN.

Tara Is Grass

THE world hath conquered, the wind hath scattered like
    dust
Alexander, Cæsar, and all that shared their sway:
Tara is grass, and behold how Troy lieth low—
And even the English, perchance their hour will come!

Translated by PADRAIC PEARSE.

Kathleen-Ni-Houlahan

L ONG they pine in weary woe, the nobles of our land,
Long they wander to and fro, proscribed, alas! and
banned;
Feastless, houseless, altarless, they bear the exile's brand,
But their hope is in the coming-to of Kathleen-Ni-Houla-
han !

Think her not a ghastly hag, too hideous to be seen,
Call her not unseemly names, our matchless Kathleen;
Young is she, and fair she is, and would be crowned a queen,
Were the King's son at home here with Kathleen-Ni-
Houlahan !

Sweet and mild would look her face, O none so sweet and
mild,
Could she crush her foes by whom her beauty is reviled;
Woollen plaids would grace herself and robes of silk her
child,
If the King's son were living here with Kathleen-Ni-
Houlahan !

Sore disgrace it is to see the Arbitress of Thrones
Vassal to a *Saxoneen* of cold and sapless bones!
Bitter anguish wrings our souls—with heavy sighs and groans
We wait the Young Deliverer of Kathleen-Ni-Houlahan !

Let us pray to Him who holds Life's issues in his hands—
Him who formed the mighty globe, with all its thousand
    lands;
Girding them with seas and mountains, rivers deep, and
    strands,
    To cast a look of pity upon Kathleen-Ni-Houlahan!

He, who over sands and waves led Israel along—
He, who fed, with heavenly bread, that chosen tribe and
    throng—
He, who stood by Moses, when his foes were fierce and
    strong—
    May He show forth His might in saving Kathleen-Ni-
    Houlahan.

            Translated by JAMES CLARENCE MANGAN.

Dark Rosaleen

O MY dark Rosaleen,
  Do not sigh, do not weep!
The priests are on the ocean green,
  They march along the deep.
There's wine from the royal Pope,
  Upon the ocean green;
And Spanish ale shall give you hope,
  My dark Rosaleen!
  My own Rosaleen!
Shall glad your heart, shall give you hope,
Shall give you health and help, and hope,
  My Dark Rosaleen.

Over hills, and through dales,
  Have I roamed for your sake;
All yesterday I sailed with sails
  On river and on lake.
The Erne, at its highest flood,
  I dashed across unseen,
For there was lightning in my blood,
  My dark Rosaleen!
  My own Rosaleen!
Oh! there was lightning in my blood,
Red lightning lightened through my blood,
  My Dark Rosaleen!

All day long in unrest,
  To and fro do I move,
The very soul within my breast
  Is wasted for you, love!
The heart in my bosom faints
  To think of you, my Queen,
My life of life, my saint of saints,
  My dark Rosaleen!
  My own Rosaleen!
To hear your sweet and sad complaints,
My life, my love, my saint of saints,
  My Dark Rosaleen!

Woe and pain, pain and woe,
  Are my lot, night and noon,
To see your bright face clouded so,
  Like to the mournful moon.
But yet will I rear your throne
  Again in golden sheen;
'Tis you shall reign, shall reign alone,
  My dark Rosaleen!
  My own Rosaleen!
'Tis you shall have the golden throne,
'Tis you shall reign, shall reign alone,
  My Dark Rosaleen!

Over dews, over sands,
  Will I fly for your weal:
Your holy, delicate white hands
  Shall girdle me with steel.
At home in your emerald bowers,
  From morning's dawn till e'en,
You'll pray for me, my flower of flowers,
  My dark Rosaleen!
  My fond Rosaleen!
You'll think of me through daylight's hours,
My virgin flower, my flower of flowers,
  My Dark Rosaleen!

I could scale the blue air,
  I could plough the high hills,
Oh, I could kneel all night in prayer,
  To heal your many ills!
And one beamy smile from you
  Would float like light between
My toils and me, my own, my true,
  My dark Rosaleen!
  My fond Rosaleen!
Would give me life and soul anew,
A second life, a soul anew,
  My Dark Rosaleen!

O! the Erne shall run red
  With redundance of blood,
The earth shall rock beneath our tread,
  And flames wrap hill and wood,
And gun-peal, and slogan cry
  Wake many a glen serene,
Ere you shall fade, ere you shall die,
  My dark Rosaleen!
  My own Rosaleen!
The Judgment Hour must first be nigh
Ere you can fade, ere you can die,
  My Dark Rosaleen!
      Translated by JAMES CLARENCE MANGAN.

Roisin Dubh

O WHO are thou with that queenly brow
   And uncrowned head?
And why is the vest that binds thy breast,
O'er the heart, blood-red?
Like a rose-bud in June that spot at noon,
A rose-bud weak;
But it deepens and grows like a July rose:
Death-pale thy cheek.

"The babes I fed at my foot lay dead;
I saw them die;
In Ramah a blast went wailing past;
It was Rachel's cry.
But I stand sublime on the shores of Time,
And I pour mine ode,
As Miriam sang to the cymbals' clang,
On the wind to God.

"Once more at my feasts my bards and priests
Shall sit and eat:
And the Shepherd whose sheep are on every steep
Shall bless my meat;
Oh, sweet, men say, is the song by day,
And the feast by night;
But on poisons I thrive, and in death survive
Through ghostly night."

AUBREY DE VERE.

The Dark Palace

THERE beams no light from thy hall to-night,
        Oh, House of Fame;
No mead-vat seethes and no smoke upwreathes
        O'er the hearth's red flame;
No high bard sings for the joy of thy kings,
        And no harpers play;
No hostage moans as thy dungeon rings
        As in Muircherteach's day.

Fallen! fallen! to ruin all in
        The covering mould;
The painted yew, and the curtains blue,
        And the cups of gold;
The linen, yellow as the corn when mellow,
        That the princes wore;
And the mirrors brazen for your queens to gaze in,
        They are here no more.

The sea-bird's pinion thatched Gormlai's grinnan;
        And through windows clear,
Without crystal pane, in her Ard-righ's reign
        She looked from here
There were quilts of eider on her couch of cedar;
        And her silken shoon
Were as green and soft as the leaves aloft
        On a bough in June.

Ah, woe unbounded where the harp once sounded
        The wind now sings;
The grey grass shivers where the mead in rivers
        Was outpoured for kings;
The min and the mether are lost together
        With the spoil of the spears;
The strong dun only has stood dark and lonely
        Through a thousand years.

But I'm not in woe for the wine-cup's flow,
        For the banquet's cheer,
For tall princesses with their trailing tresses
        And their broidered gear;
My grief and my trouble for this palace noble
        With no chief to lead
'Gainst the Saxon stranger on the day of danger
        Out of Aileach Neid.
                ALICE MILLIGAN.

After Death

SHALL mine eyes behold thy glory, oh, my country?
  Shall mine eyes behold thy glory?
Or shall the darkness close around them ere the sun-blaze
  Break at last upon thy story?

When the nations ope for thee their queenly circle,
  As sweet new sister hail thee,
Shall these lips be sealed in callous death and silence,
  That have known but to bewail thee?

Shall the ear be deaf that only loved thy praises,
  When all men their tribute bring thee?
Shall the mouth be clay that sang thee in thy squalor,
  When all poets' mouths shall sing thee?

Ah! the harpings and the salvos and the shoutings
  Of thy exiled sons returning,
I should hear, tho' dead and mouldered, and the grave-damps
  Should not chill my bosom's burning.

Ah! the tramp of feet victorious! I should hear them
  'Mid the shamrocks and the mosses,
And my heart should toss within the shroud and quiver
  As a captive dreamer tosses.

I should turn and rend the cere-cloths round me—
  Giant sinews I should borrow—
Crying, "Oh, my brothers, I have also loved her
  In her loneliness and sorrow!

"Let me join with you the jubilant procession,
  Let me chant with you her story;
Then, contented, I shall go back to the shamrocks,
  Now mine eyes have seen her glory!"

FANNY PARNELL.

Ways of War

A TERRIBLE and splendid trust,
   Heartens the host of Innisfail;
Their dream is of the swift sword-thrust;
   The lightning glory of the Gael.

Croagh Patrick is the place of prayers,
   And Tara the assembling place:
But each sweet wind of Ireland bears
   The trump of battle on its race.

From Dursey Isle to Donegal,
   From Howth to Achill, the glad noise
Rings: and the airs of glory fall,
   Or victory crowns their fighting joys.

A dream! a dream! an ancient dream!
   Yet, ere peace come to Innisfail,
Some weapons on some field must gleam,
   Some burning glory fire the Gael.

That field may lie beneath the sun,
   Fair for the treading of an host:
That field in realms of thought be won
   And armed minds do their uttermost.

Some way, to faithful Innisfail,
   Shall come the majesty and awe
Of martial truth, that must prevail,
   To lay on all the eternal law.
LIONEL JOHNSON.

This Heritage to the Race of Kings

THIS heritage to the race of kings,
  Their children and their children's seed
Have wrought their prophecies in deed
Of terrible and splendid things.

The hands that fought, the hearts that broke
In old immortal tragedies,
These have not failed beneath the skies,
Their children's heads refuse the yoke.

And still their hands shall guard the sod
That holds their father's funeral urn,
Still shall their hearts volcanic burn
With anger of the sons of God.

No alien sword shall earn as wage
The entail of their blood and tears,
No shameful price for peaceful years
Shall ever part this heritage.

JOSEPH PLUNKETT.

The Irish Rapparees

R IGH SHEMUS he has gone to France, and left his crown
     behind;
Ill luck be theirs, both day and night, put running in his
     mind
Lord Lucan followed after, with his Slashers brave and true,
And now the doleful keen is raised—"What will poor Ireland
     do?
What must poor Ireland do?
Our luck," they say, "has gone to France—what can poor
     Ireland do?"

Oh! never fear for Ireland, for she has soldiers still;
For Rory's boys are in the wood, and Remy's on the hill;
And never had poor Ireland more loyal hearts than these—
May God be kind and good to them, the faithful Rapparees
The fearless Rapparees!
The jewel were you, Rory, with your Irish Rapparees!

Oh, black's your heart, Clan Oliver, and colder than the clay!
Oh, high's your head, Clan Sassenach, since Sarsfield's gone
     away!
It's little love you bear to us, for the sake of long ago
But hold your hand, for Ireland still can strike a deadly
     blow—
Can strike a mortal blow—
Och, dar-a-Críost 'tis she that still
Could strike a deadly blow.

The Master's bawn, the Master's seat, a surly bodagh fills;
The Master's son, an outlawed man, is riding on the hills.
But God be praised that round him throng, as thick as summer bees,
The swords that guarded Limerick wall—his faithful Rapparees!
His loving Rapparees!
Who dare say "no" to Rory Oge, with all his Rapparees?

Black Billy Grimes of Latnamard, he racked us long and sore—
God rest the faithful hearts he broke!—we'll never see them more
But I'll go bail he'll break no more, while Truagh has gallows trees;
For why?—he met one lonely night, the fearless Rapparees
The angry Rapparees!
They never sin no more, my boys, who cross the Rapparees.

Now, Sassenach and Cromweller, take heed of what I say—
Keep down your black and angry looks, that scorn us night and day:
For there's a just and wrathful Judge, that every action sees,
And He'll make strong, to right our wrong, the faithful Rapparees!
The fearless Rapparees!
The men that rode by Sarsfield's side, the roving Rapparees!
CHARLES GAVAN DUFFY.

The Memory of the Dead

WHO fears to speak of Ninety-Eight?
  Who blushes at the name?
When cowards mock the patriot's fate,
Who hangs his head for shame?
He's all a knave, or half a slave,
Who slights his country thus;
But a true man, like, you, man,
Will fill your glass with us.

We drink the memory of the brave,
The faithful and the few:
Some lie far off beyond the wave,
Some sleep in Ireland, too;
All, all are gone; but still lives on
The fame of those who died;
All true men, like you, men,
Remember them with pride.

Some on the shores of distant lands
Their weary hearts have laid,
And by the stranger's heedless hands
Their lonely graves were made;
But, though their clay be far away
Beyond the Atlantic foam,
In true men, like you, men,
Their spirit's still at home.

The dust of some is Irish earth,
Among their own they rest,
And the same land that gave them birth
Has caught them to her breast;
And we will pray that from their clay
Full many a race may start
Of true men, like you, men,
To act as brave a part.

They rose in dark and evil days
To right their native land;
They kindled here a living blaze
That nothing shall withstand.
Alas! that Might can vanquish Right—
They fell and passed away;
But true men, like you, men,
Are plenty here to-day.

Then here's to their memory—may it be
For us a guiding light,
To hear our strife for liberty,
And teach us to unite—
Through good and ill, be Ireland's still,
Though sad as theirs your fate,
And true men, be you, men,
Like those of Ninety-Eight.
                    JOHN KELLY INGRAM.

Thro' Grief and Thro' Danger

THRO' grief and thro' danger thy smile hath cheer'd my
    way,
Till hope seem'd to bud from each thorn that round me lay;
The darker our fortune, the brighter our pure love burned,
Till shame into glory, till fear into zeal was turned,
Oh! slave as I was, in thy arms my spirit felt free,
And bless'd e'en the sorrows that made me more dear to thee.

Thy rival was honoured, while thou wert wronged and
    scorned;
Thy crown was of briers, while gold her brows adorned;
She woo'd me to temples, while thou lay'st hid in caves;
Her friends were all masters, while thine, alas! were slaves;
Yet, cold in the earth at thy feet I would rather be,
Than wed what I lov'd not, or turn one thought from thee.

THOMAS MOORE.

The Irish Mother in the Penal Days

NOW welcome, welcome, baby-boy, unto a mother's fears,
The pleasure of her sufferings, the rainbow of her tears,
The object of your father's hope, in all he hopes to do,
A future man of his own land, to live him o'er anew!

How fondly on thy little brow a mother's eye would trace.
And in thy little limbs, and in each feature of thy face,
His beauty, worth, and manliness, and everything that's his,
Except, my boy, the answering mark of where the fetter is!

Oh! many a weary hundred years his sires that fetter wore,
And he has worn it since the day that him his mother bore;
And now, my son, it waits on you, the moment you are born:
The old hereditary badge of suffering and scorn!

Alas, my boy, so beautiful!—alas, my love so brave!
And must your gallant Irish limbs still drag it to the grave?
And you, my son, yet have a son, foredoomed a slave to be,
Whose mother still must weep o'er him the tears I weep o'er
    thee!

JOHN BANIM.

A Song of Freedom

IN CAVAN of little lakes,
  As I was walking with the w
And no one seen beside me ther
  There came a song into my mi
It came as if the whispered voic
  Of one, but none of human kin
Who walked with me in Cavan t
  And he invisible as wind.

On Urris of Inish-Owen,
  As I went up the mountain sid
The brook that came leaping dow
  Cried to me—for joy it cried;
And when from off the summit fa
  I looked o'er land and water w
I was more joyous than the bro
  That met me on the mountain

To Ara of Connacht's isles,
  As I went sailing o'er the sea
The wind's word, the brook's wo
  The wave's word, was plain to
As we are, though she is not,
  As we are, shall Banba be—
There is no king can rule the wi
  There is no fetter for the sea.

ALICE MILLIGA

285

Terence MacSwiney

SEE, though the oil be low more purely still and higher
  The flame burns in the body's lamp! The watchers still
Gaze with unseeing eyes while the Promethean Will,
The Uncreated Light, the Everlasting Fire
Sustains itself against the torturer's desire
Even as the fabled Titan chained upon the hill.
Burn on, shine on, thou immortality, until
We, too, have lit our lamps at the funereal pyre;
Till we, too, can be noble, unshakable, undismayed:
Till we, too, can burn with the holy flame, and know
There is that within us can triumph over pain,
And go to death, alone, slowly, and unafraid.
The candles of God are already burning row on row:
Farewell, lightbringer, fly to thy heaven again!

A. E.

The Three Woes

THAT angel whose charge was Eiré sang thus, o'er the
    dark Isle winging;
By a virgin his song was heard at a tempest's ruinous close:
"Three golden ages God gave while your tender green blade
    was springing;
Faith's earliest harvest is reaped. To-day God sends you
    three woes.

"For ages three without laws ye shall flee as beasts in the
    forest;
For an age and a half age faith shall bring, not peace, but a
    sword;
Then laws shall rend you, like eagles sharp-fanged, of your
    scourges the sorest;
When these three woes are past, look up, for your hope is
    restored.

"The times of your woes shall be twice the time of your
    foregone glory;
But fourfold at last shall lie the grain on your granary
    floor."
The seas in vapour shall flee, and in ashes the mountains
    hoary;
Let God do that which He wills. Let his servants endure
    and adore!"

AUBREY DE VERE.

PART VII
PERSONAL POEMS

I Am Raferty

I AM Raferty the Poet
    Full of hope and love,
With eyes that have no light,
    With gentleness that has no misery.

Going west upon my pilgrimage
    By the light of my heart,
Feeble and tired
    To the end of my road.

Behold me now,
    And my face to the wall,
A-playing music
    Unto empty pockets.

                    Translated by DOUGLAS HYDE.

At the Mid Hour of Night

A T THE mid hour of night, when stars are weeping, I fly
to the lone vale we loved, when life shone warm in
thine eye ;
And I think oft, if spirits can steal from the regions of air,
To revisit past scenes of delight, thou wilt come to me there,
And tell me our love is remembered, even in the sky.

Then I sing the wild song 'twas once such pleasure to hear
When our voices commingling breathed, like one, on the ear;
And, as Echo far off through the vale my sad orison rolls,
I think, oh, my love! 'tis thy voice from the Kingdom of
Souls,
Faintly answering still the notes that once were so dear.

THOMAS MOORE.

Night

MYSTERIOUS Night! When our first parent knew
Thee, from report divine, and heard thy name,
Did he not tremble for this lovely Frame,
This glorious canopy of Light and Blue?
Yet, 'neath a curtain of translucent dew,
Bathed in the rays of the great setting Flame,
Hesperus, with the Host of Heaven, came,
And lo! Creation widened on Man's view.

Who could have thought such darkness lay concealed
Within thy beams, O Sun! or who could find,
Whilst flower and leaf and insect stood revealed,
That to such countless orbs thou mad'st us blind!
Why do we then shun Death with anxious strife?
If Light can thus deceive, wherefore not Life?

JOSEPH BLANCO WHITE.

Nepenthe

O BLEST unfabled Incense Tree,
   That burns in glorious Araby,
With red scent chalicing the air,
Till earth-life grow Elysian there!

Half buried to her flaming breast
In this bright tree she makes her nest,
Hundred-sunned Phœnix! when she must
Crumble at length to hoary dust;

Her gorgeous death-bed, her rich pyre
Burnt up with aromatic fire;
Her urn, sight-high from spoiler men,
Her birthplace when self-born again.

The mountainless green wilds among,
Here ends she her unechoing song:
With amber tears and odorous sighs
Mourned by the desert where she dies.
                    GEORGE DARLEY.

Eileen Aroon

WHEN, like the early rose,
   Eileen aroon!
Beauty in childhood blows,
   Eileen aroon!
When, like a diadem,
Buds blush around the stem,
Which is the fairest gem?
   Eileen aroon!

Is it the laughing eye,
   Eileen aroon!
Is it the timid sigh,
   Eileen aroon!
Is it the tender tone,
Soft as the stringed harp's moan?
Oh! it is Truth alone.
   Eileen aroon!

When, like the rising day,
   Eileen aroon!
Love sends his early ray,
   Eileen aroon!
What makes his dawning glow
Changeless through joy or woe?
Only the constant know—
   Eileen aroon!

I know a valley fair,
    Eileen aroon!
I knew a cottage there,
    Eileen aroon!
Far in that valley shade
I knew a gentle maid,
Flower of a hazel glade,
    Eileen aroon!

Who in the song so sweet?
    Eileen aroon!
Who in the dance so fleet?
    Eileen aroon!
Dear were her charms to me,
Dearer her laughter free,
Dearest her constancy,
    Eileen aroon!

Were she no longer true,
    Eileen aroon!
What should her lover do?
    Eileen aroon!
Fly with his broken chain
Far o'er the sounding main,
Never to love again,
    Eileen aroon!

Youth must with time decay,
    Eileen aroon!
Beauty must fade away,
    Eileen aroon!
Castles are sacked in war,
Chieftains are scattered far,
Truth is a fixed star,
    Eileen aroon!
                GERALD GRIFFIN.

And Then No More

I SAW her once, one little while, and then no more:
   'Twas Eden's light on Earth a while, and then no more.
Amid the throng she passed along the meadow-floor:
Spring seemed to smile on Earth awhile, and then no more;
But whence she came, which way she went, what garb she
      wore
I noted not; I gazed a while, and then no more!

I saw her once, one little while, and then no more:
'Twas Paradise on Earth a while, and then no more.
Ah! what avail my vigils pale, my magic lore?
She shone before mine eyes awhile, and then no more.
The shallop of my peace is wrecked on Beauty's shore.
Near Hope's fair isle it rode awhile, and then no more!

I saw her once, one little while, and then no more:
Earth looked like Heaven a little while, and then no more.
Her presence thrilled and lighted to its inner core
My desert breast a little while, and then no more.
So may, perchance, a meteor glance at midnight o'er
Some ruined pile a little while, and then no more!

I saw her once, one little while, and then no more:
The earth was Peri-land awhile, and then no more.
Oh, might I see but once again, as once before,
Through chance or wile, that shape awhile, and then no
      more!
Death soon would heal my griefs! This heart, now sad and
      sore,
Would beat anew a little while, and then no more.

                              JAMES CLARENCE MANGAN.

297

Maire My Girl

OVER the dim blue hills
  Strays a wild river,
Over the dim blue hills
Rests my heart ever.
Dearer and brighter than
Jewels and pearl,
Dwells she in beauty there,
Maire my girl.

Down upon Claris heath
Shines the soft berry,
On the brown harvest tree
Droops the red cherry.
Sweeter thy honey lips,
Softer the curl
Straying adown thy cheeks,
Maire my girl.

'Twas on an April eve
That I first met her;
Many an eve shall pass
Ere I forget her.
Since my young heart has been
Wrapped in a whirl,
Thinking and dreaming of
Maire my girl.

She is too kind and fond
Ever to grieve me,
She has too pure a heart
E'er to deceive me.
Was I Tyrconnell's chief
Or Desmond's earl,
Life would be dark, wanting
Maire my girl.

Over the dim blue hills
Strays a wild river,
Over the dim blue hills
Rests my heart ever;
Dearer and brighter than
Jewels or pearl,
Dwells she in beauty there,
Maire my girl.
        JOHN KEEGAN CASEY.

Helas!

TO drift with every passion till my soul
 Is as a stringed lute on which all winds can play,
Is it for this that I have given away
Mine ancient wisdom and austere control?
Methinks my life is a twice-written scroll
Scrawled over on some boyish holiday
With idle songs for pipe and virelay,
Which do but mar the secret of the whole.

Surely there was a time I might have trod
The sunlit heights, and from life's dissonance
Struck one clear chord to reach the ears of God:
Is that time dead? Lo! with a little rod
I did but touch the honey of romance—
And must I lose my soul's inheritance?

OSCAR WILDE.

In the Streets of Catania

("The streets of Catania are paved with blocks of the lava
of Ætna")

ALL that was beautiful and just,
  All that was pure and sad
Went in one little, moving plot of dust
The world called bad.

Came like a highwayman, and went,
One who was bold and gay,
Left when his lightly loving mood was spent
Thy heart to pay.

By-word of little street and men,
Narrower theirs the shame,
Tread thou the lava loving leaves, and then
Turn whence it came.

Ætna, all wonderful, whose heart
Glows as thine throbbing glows,
Almond and citron bloom quivering at start,
Ends in pure snows.

ROGER CASEMENT.

The Doves

THE house where I was born,
　　Where I was young and gay,
Grows old amid its corn,
Amid its scented hay.

Moan of the cushat dove,
In silence rich and deep;
The old head I love
Nods to its quiet sleep.

Where once were nine and ten
Now two keep house together;
The doves moan and complain
All day in the still weather.

What wind, bitter and great,
Has swept the country's face,
Altered, made desolate
The heart-remembered place?

What wind, bitter and wild,
Has swept the towering trees
Beneath whose shade a child
Long since gathered heartease?

Under the golden eaves
The house is still and sad,
As though it grieves and grieves
For many a lass and lad.

The cushat doves complain
All day in the still weather;
Where once were nine or ten
But two keep house together.
KATHERINE TYNAN.

Sheep and Lambs

ALL in the April evening,
April airs were abroad;
The sheep with their little lambs
Passed me by on the road.

The sheep with their little lambs
Passed me by on the road;
All in the April evening
I thought on the Lamb of God.

The lambs were weary and crying
With a weak, human cry.
I thought on the Lamb of God
Going meekly to die.

Up in the blue, blue mountains
Dewy pastures are sweet;
Rest for the little bodies,
Rest for the little feet.

But for the Lamb of God,
Up on the hill-top green,
Only a cross of shame
Two stark crosses between.

All in the April evening,
April airs were abroad;
I saw the sheep with their lambs,
And thought on the Lamb of God.
                KATHERINE TYNAN.

The Pity of Love

A PITY beyond all telling
  Is hid in the heart of love:
The folk who are buying and selling,
The clouds on their journey above,
The cold, wet winds ever blowing,
And the shadowy hazel grove
Where mouse-grey waters are flowing
Threaten the head that I love.
WILLIAM BUTLER YEATS.

The Folly of Being Comforted

ONE that is ever kind said yesterday:
   "Your well beloved's hair has threads of grey,
And little shadows come about her eyes;
Time can but make it easier to be wise,
Though now it's hard, till trouble is at an end;
And so be patient, be wise and patient, friend."
But heart, there is no comfort, not a grain;
Time can but make her beauty over again,
Because of that great nobleness of hers;
The fire that stirs about her, when she stirs
Burns but more clearly. O she had not these ways,
When all the wild Summer was in her gaze.
O heart! O heart! if she'd but turn her head,
You'd know the folly of being comforted.
WILLIAM BUTLER YEATS.

Think

THINK, the ragged turf-boy urges
  O'er the dusty road his asses;
Think, on the seashore far the lonely
Heron wings along the sand.
Think, in woodland under oak-boughs
Now the streaming sunbeam passes:
And bethink thee thou art servant
To the same all-moving hand.

CHARLES WEEKS.

Immortality

WE MUST pass like smoke or live within the spirit's fire;
    For we can no more than smoke unto the flame return
If our thought has changed to dream, our will unto desire,
    As smoke we vanish though the fire may burn.

Lights of infinite pity star the grey dusk of our days:
Surely here is soul: with it we have eternal breath:
In the fire of love we live, or pass by many ways,
    By unnumbered ways of dream to death.

"A. E."

A Farewell

I GO down from the hill in gladness, and half with a pain I
    depart,
Where the Mother with gentlest breathing made music on lip
    and in heart;
For I know that my childhood is over: a call comes out of
    the vast,
And the love that I had in the old time, like beauty in twi-
    light, is past.

I am fired by a Danaan whisper of battles afar in the world,
And my thought is no longer of peace, for the banners in
    dream are unfurled,
And I pass from the council of stars and of hills to a life
    that is new:
And I bid to you stars and you mountains a tremulous long
    adieu.

I will come once again as a master, who played here as a
    child in my dawn;
I will enter the heart of the hills where the gods of the old
    world are gone.
And will war like the bright Hound of Ulla with princes of
    earth and of sky.
For my dream is to conquer the heavens and battle for king-
    ship on high.

"A. E."

To Morfydd

A VOICE on the winds,
 A voice by the waters,
Wanders and cries:
Oh! what are the winds?
And what are the waters?
 Mine are your eyes!

Western the winds are,
And western the waters,
 Where the light lies:
Oh! what are the winds?
And what are the waters?
 Mine are your eyes!

Cold, cold, grow the winds,
And wild grow the waters,
 Where the sun dies:
Oh! what are the winds?
And what are the waters?
 Mine are your eyes!

And down the night winds,
And down the night waters,
 The music flies:
Oh! what are the winds?
And what are the waters?
Cold be the winds,
And wild be the waters,
 So mine be your eyes!
 LIONEL JOHNSON.

Love on the Mountain

MY LOVE comes down from the mountain
  Through the mists of dawn;
I look, and the star of the morning
From the sky is gone.

My love comes down from the mountain,
At dawn, dewy-sweet;
Did you step from the star to the mountain,
O little white feet?

O whence came your twining tresses
And your shining eyes,
But out of the gold of the morning
And the blue of the skies?

The misty morning is burning
In the sun's red fire,
And the heart in my breast is burning
And lost in desire.

I follow you into the valley
But no word can I say;
To the East or the West I will follow
Till the dusk of my day.

THOMAS BOYD.

Night's Ancient Cloud

S HALLOW dark but mocks the eyes.
Shallow dark has no surprise.
Deeper darkness deifies.

Light we see and feel is fled,
Flakeless as a phantom sped.
Mystery on mystery shed,—
It must die to raise its head.

At its death old time is still.
Space, enthralled with stars that spill,
Waiteth tremblingly, until

Light grown weary of its shroud,
Leaps alive with crest unbowed,
Revels in night's ancient cloud.

THOMAS KEOHLER.

Mad Song

I HEAR the wind a-blowing,
   I hear the corn a-growing,
I hear the Virgin praying,
I hear what she is saying!
        HESTER SIGERSON.

The Wings of Love

I WILL row my boat on Muckross Lake when the grey of
    the dove
Comes down at the end of the day; and a quiet like prayer
Grows soft in your eyes, and among your fluttering hair
The red of the sun is mixed with the red of your cheek.
I will row you, O boat of my heart! till our mouths have for-
    gotten to speak
In the silence of love, broken only by trout that spring
And are gone, like a fairy's finger that casts a ring
With the luck of the world for the hand that can hold it fast.
I will rest on my oars, my eyes on your eyes, till our thoughts
    have passed
From the lake and the sky and the rings of the jumping fish;
Till our ears are filled from the reeds with a sudden swish,
And a sound like the beating of flails in the time of corn.
We shall hold our breath while a wonderful thing is born
From the songs that were chanted by bards in the days gone
    by;
For a wild white swan shall be leaving the lake for the sky,
With the curve of her neck stretched out in a silver spear.
Oh! then when the creak of her wings shall have brought
    her near,
We shall hear again a swish, and a beating of flails,
And a creaking of oars, and a sound like the wind in sails,
As the mate of her heart shall follow her into the air.
O wings of my soul! we shall think of Angus and Caer,
And Etain and Midir, that were changed into wild white
    swans

To fly round the ring of the heavens, through the dusks and
the dawns,
Unseen by all but true lovers, till judgment day,
Because they had loved for love only. O love! I will say,
For a woman and man with eternity ringing them round,
And the heavens above and below them, a poor thing it is to
be bound
To four low walls that will spill like a pedlar's pack,
And a quilt that will run into holes, and a churn that will
dry and crack.
Oh! better than these, a dream in the night, or our heart's
mute prayer
That O'Donoghue, the enchanted man, should pass between
water and air,
And say, I will change them each to a wild white swan,
Like the lovers Angus and Midir, and their loved ones, Caer
and Etain,
Because they have loved for love only, and have searched
through the shadows of things
For the Heart of all hearts, through the fire of love, and the
wine of love, and the wings.

JAMES H. COUSINS.

On a Poet Patriot

HIS songs were a little phrase
  Of eternal song,
Drowned in the harping of lays
  More loud and long.

His deed was a single word,
  Called out alone
In a night when no echo stirred
  To laughter or moan.

But his songs new souls shall thrill,
  The loud harps dumb,
And his deed the echoes fill
  When the dawn is come.
              THOMAS MACDONAGH.

Wishes for My Son

Born on Saint Cecilia's Day, 1912

NOW, my son, is life for you,
     And I wish you joy of it,—
Joy of power in all you do,
Deeper passion, better wit
Than I had who had enough,
Quicker life and length thereof,
More of every gift but love.

Love I have beyond all men,
Love that now you share with me—
What have I to wish you then
But that you be good and free,
And that God to you may give
Grace in stronger days to live?

For I wish you more than I
Ever knew of glorious deed,
Though no rapture passed me by
That an eager heart could heed,
Though I followed heights and sought
Things the sequel never brought.

Wild and perilous holy things
Flaming with a martyr's blood,
And the joy that laughs and sings
Where a foe must be withstood,
Joy of headlong happy chance
Leading on the battle dance.

But I found no enemy,
No man in a world of wrong,
That Christ's word of charity
Did not render clean and strong—
Who was I to judge my kind,
Blindest groper of the blind?

God to you may give the sight
And the clear, undoubting strength
Wars to knit for single right,
Freedom's war to knit at length,
And to win through wrath and strife,
To the sequel of my life.

But for you, so small and young,
Born on Saint Cecilia's Day,
I in more harmonious song
Now for nearer joys should pray—
Simpler joys: the natural growth
Of your childhood and your youth,
Courage, innocence, and truth:

These for you, so small and young,
In your hand and heart and tongue.
                    THOMAS MACDONAGH.

Greeting

OVER the wave-patterned sea-floor,
  Over the long sunburnt ridge of the world,
I bid the winds seek you.
I bid them cry to you
Night and morning
A name you loved once;
I bid them bring to you
Dreams, and strange imaginings, and sleep.

ELLA YOUNG.

319

The Sedges

I WHISPERED my great sorrow
  To every listening sedge;
And they bent, bowed with my sorrow,
  Down to the water's edge.

But she stands and laughs lightly
  To see me sorrow so,
Like the light winds that laughing
  Across the water go.

If I could tell the bright ones
  That quiet-hearted move,
They would bend down like the sedges
  With the sorrow of love.

But she stands laughing lightly,
  Who all my sorrow knows,
Like the little wind that laughing
  Across the water blows.
                    SEUMAS O'SULLIVAN

The Half Door

DARK eyes, wonderful, strange and dear they shone
    A moment's space;
And wandering under the white stars I had gone
    In a strange place.

Over the half door careless, your white hand
    A moment gleamed;
And I was walking on some great storm-heaped strand
    Forever it seemed.

I would give all that glory to see once more,
    A moment's space,
Your eyes gleam strange and dark above the half door,
    Your hand's white grace.

                        Seumas O'Sullivan.

This Heart That Flutters Near My Heart

THIS heart that flutters near my heart
　　My hope and all my riches is,
Unhappy when we draw apart
　　And happy between kiss and kiss;
My hope and all my riches—yes!—
　　And all my happiness.

For there, as in some mossy nest
　　The wrens will divers treasures keep,
I laid those treasures I possessed
　　Ere that mine eyes had learned to weep.
Shall we not be as wise as they
　　Though love live but a day?

JAMES JOYCE.

I Hear an Army

I HEAR an army charging upon the land,
   And the thunder of horses plunging, foam about their
      knees:
Arrogant, in black armour, behind them stand,
Disdaining the reins, with fluttering whips, the charioteers.

They cry unto the night their battle-name:
I moan in sleep when I hear afar their whirling laughter.
They cleave the gloom of dreams, a blinding flame,
Clanging, clanging upon my heart as upon an anvil.

They come shaking in triumph their long, green hair:
They come out of the sea and run shouting by the shore.
My heart, have you no wisdom thus to despair?
My love, my love, my love, why have you left me alone?

JAMES JOYCE.

To Death

I HAVE not gathered gold;
  The fame that I won perished;
In love I found but sorrow,
  That withered my life.

Of wealth or of glory
I shall leave nothing behind me
(I think it, O God, enough!)
  But my name in the heart of a child.
                    PADRAIC PEARSE.
          Translated by Thomas MacDonagh.

Ideal

NAKED I saw thee,
　　O beauty of beauty!
And I blinded my eyes
For fear I should flinch.

I heard thy music,
O sweetness of sweetness!
And I shut my ears
For fear I should fail.

I kissed thy lips
O sweetness of sweetness!
And I hardened my heart
For fear of my ruin.

I blinded my eyes
And my ears I shut,
I hardened my heart
And my love I quenched.

I turned my back
On the dream I had shaped,
And to this road before me
My face I turned.

I set my face
To the road here before me,
To the work that I see,
To the death that I shall meet.
　　　　　　PADRAIC PEARSE.
　　　　　Translated by Thomas MacDonagh.

River-Mates

I'LL be an otter, and I'll let you swim
  A mate beside me; we will venture down
A deep, dark river, when the sky above
Is shut of the sun; spoilers are we,
Thick-coated; no dog's tooth can bite at our veins,
With eyes and ears of poachers; deep-earthed ones
Turned hunters; let him slip past
The little vole; my teeth are on an edge
For the King-fish of the River!

      I hold him up
The glittering salmon that smells of the sea;
I hold him high and whistle!
      Now we go
Back to our earths; we will tear and eat
Sea-smelling salmon; you will tell the cubs
I am the Booty-bringer, I am the Lord
Of the River; the deep, dark, full and flowing River!

PADRAIC COLUM.

The Betrayal

WHEN you were weary, roaming the wide world over,
   I gave my fickle heart to a new lover.
Now they tell me that you are lying dead:
O mountains fall on me and hide my head!

When you lay burning in the throes of fever,
He vowed me love by the willow-margined river:
Death smote you there—here was your trust betrayed,
O darkness, cover me, I am afraid!

Yea, in the hour of your supremest trial,
I laughed with him! The shadows on the dial
Stayed not, aghast at my dread ignorance:
Nor man nor angel looked at me askance.

.   .   .   .

Under the mountains there is peace abiding,
Darkness shall be pavilion for my hiding,
Tears shall blot out the sin of broken faith,
The lips that falsely kissed, shall kiss but Death.

                                        ALICE FURLONG.

The Daisies

IN THE scented bud of the morning—O,
  When the windy grass went rippling
    far,
I saw my dear one walking slow,
  In the field where the daisies are.

We did not laugh and we did not speak
  As we wandered happily to and fro;
I kissed my dear on either cheek,
  In the bud of the morning—O.

A lark sang up from the breezy land,
  A lark sang down from a cloud afar,
And she and I went hand in hand
  In the field where the daisies are.
JAMES STEPHENS.

The Goat Paths

THE crooked paths go every way
    Upon the hill—they wind about
Through the heather in and out
Of the quiet sunniness.
And there the goats, day after day,
Stray in sunny quietness,
Cropping here and cropping there,
As they pause and turn and pass,
Now a bit of heather spray,
Now a mouthful of the grass.

In the deeper sunniness,
In the place where nothing stirs,
Quietly in quietness,
In the quiet of the furze,
For a time they come and lie
Staring on the roving sky.

If you approach they run away,
They leap and stare, away they bound,
With a sudden angry sound,
To the sunny quietude;
Crouching down where nothing stirs
In the silence of the furze,
Crouching down again to brood
In the sunny solitude.

If I were as wise as they,
I would stray apart and brood,
I would beat a hidden way
Through the quiet heather spray
To a sunny solitude;

And should you come I'd run away,
I would make an angry sound,
I would stare and turn and bound
To the deeper quietude,
To the place where nothing stirs
In the silence of the furze.

In that airy quietness
I would think as long as they;
Through the quiet sunniness
I would stray away to brood
By a hidden, beaten way
In the sunny solitude.

I would think until I found
Something I can never find,
Something lying on the ground,
In the bottom of my mind.

JAMES STEPHENS.

The Spark

BECAUSE I used to shun
    Death and the mouth of hell
And count my battles won
If I should see the sun
The blood and smoke dispel.

Because I used to pray
That living I might see
The dawning light of day
Set me upon my way
And from my fetters free,
Because I used to seek
Your answer to my prayer
And that your soul should speak
For strengthening of the weak
To struggle with despair,

Now I have seen my shame
That I should thus deny
My soul's divinest flame,
Now shall I shout your name,
Now shall I seek to die

By any hands but these
In battle or in flood,
On any lands or seas,
No more shall I spare ease,
No more shall I spare blood

When I have need to fight
For heaven or for your heart,

Against the powers of light
Or darkness I shall smite
Until their might depart,

Because I know the spark
Of God has no eclipse,
Now Death and I embark
And sail into the dark
With laughter on our lips.

JOSEPH PLUNKETT.

A Soft Day

A SOFT day, thank God!
  A wind from the south
With honeyed mouth;
A scent of drenching leaves,
Briar and beech and lime,
White elder-flower and thyme
And the soaking grass smells sweet
Crushed by my two bare feet,
While the rain drips,
Drips, drips, drips from the eaves.

A soft day, thank God!
The hills wear a shroud
Of silver cloud;
The web the spider weaves
Is a glittering net;
The woodland path is wet,
And the soaking earth smells sweet
Under my two bare feet,
And the rain drips,
Drips, drips, drips from the leaves.

WINIFRED M. LETTS.

He Whom a Dream Hath Possessed

HE WHOM a dream hath possessed knoweth no more of
    doubting,
For mist and the blowing of winds and the mouthing of
    words he scorns;
Not the sinuous speech of schools he hears, but a knightly
    shouting,
And never comes darkness down, yet he greeteth a million
    morns.

He whom a dream hath possessed knoweth no more of roam-
    ing;
All roads and the flowing of waves and the speediest flight
    he knows,
But wherever his feet are set, his soul is forever homing,
And going he comes, and coming he heareth a call and goes.

He whom a dream hath possessed knoweth no more of sorrow,
At death and the dropping of leaves and the fading of suns
    he smiles,
For a dream remembers no past and scorns the desire of a
    morrow,
And a dream in a sea of doom sets surely the ultimate isles.

He whom a dream hath possessed treads the impalpable
    marches,
From the dust of the day's long road he leaps to a laughing
    star,
And the ruin of worlds that fall he views from eternal arches,
And rides God's battlefield in a flashing and golden car.

SHAEMAS O'SHEEL

The Wind Bloweth Where It Listeth

MY HEART lies light in my own breast
That yesterday in yours found rest.

Indeed, beloved, I would stay
With you to-day as yesterday;

But oh! the being comes and goes,
The spirit is a wind that blows.

Though lip to lip no more we press
Our spirits feel that tenderness

That woke within us here and fled
To its own heaven overhead.

It sits there in a starry place,
With looks of longing on its face

And beckons us to mount and find
The love that fled upon the wind.

Not the old wayward child to see
But some bright-haired divinity.

SUSAN L. MITCHELL.

The Apple-Tree

I SAW the archangels in my apple-tree last night,
   I saw them like great birds in the starlight—
Purple and burning blue, crimson and shining white.

And each to each they tossed an apple to and fro,
And once I heard their laughter gay and low;
And yet I felt no wonder that it should be so.

But when the apple came one time to Michael's lap
I heard him say: "The mysteries that enwrap
The earth and fill the heavens can be read here, mayhap."

Then Gabriel spoke: "I praise the deed, the hidden thing."
"The beauty of the blossom of the spring
I praise," cried Raphael. Uriel: "The wise leaves I sing."

And Michael: "I will praise the fruit, perfected, round,
Full of the love of God, herein being bound
His mercies gathered from the sun and rain and ground."

So sang they till a small wind through the branches stirred,
And spoke of coming dawn; and at its word
Each fled away to heaven, winged like a bird.

NANCY CAMPBELL.

PART VIII
POEMS SINCE 1920

Aisling

AT MORNING from the coldness of Mount Brandon,
The sail is blowing half-way to the light;
And islands are so small, a man may carry
Their yellow crop in one cart at low tide.
Sadly in thought, I strayed the mountain grass
To hear the breezes following their young
And by the furrow of a stream, I chanced
To find a woman airing in the sun.

Coil of her hair, in cluster and ringlet,
Had brightened round her forehead and those curls—
Closer than she could bind them on a finger—
Were changing gleam and glitter. O she turned
So gracefully aside, I thought her clothes
Were flame and shadow while she slowly walked,
Or that each breast was proud because it rode
The cold air as the wave stayed by the swan.

But knowing her face was fairer than in thought,
I asked of her was she the Geraldine—
Few horsemen sheltered at the steps of water?
Or that Greek woman, lying in a piled room
On tousled purple, whom the household saved,
When frescoes of strange fire concealed the pillar:
The white coin all could spend? Might it be Niav
And was she over wave or from our hills?

"When shadows in wet grass are heavier
Than hay, beside dim wells the women gossip
And by the paler bushes tell the daylight;
But from what bay, uneasy with a shipping
Breeze, have you come?" I said. "O do you cross
The blue thread and the crimson on the framework,
At darkfall in a house where nobles throng
And the slow oil climbs up into the flame?"

"Black and fair strangers leave upon the oar
And there is peace," she answered. "Companies
Are gathered in the house that I have known;
Claret is on the board and they are pleased
By story-telling. When the turf is redder
And airy packs of wonder have been told,
My women dance to bright steel that is wed,
Starlike, upon the anvil with one stroke."

AUSTIN CLARKE.

Dirge of the Lone Woman

A S WE entered by that door
    We saw the lights a-flame—
A-flame on your bier,
On the bier of you
Who had loved many a one,
Loved many a one!

Then I said to your love,
To her, your latest love,
'There's his last room,
His final roof-tree
Who has lived in many a one,
In many a one.

'A tree never more
Grows to shield him
From the bitter cold and rain,
From the blighting light of love
Which ends many a one—
Ends many a one.

'There's his last tree;
You're his last love:
The new bud in bloom,
The new fruit of the flower
He'll give to no other one,
To no other one!'

Then they raised up your bier,
They quenched the laggard flame,
And they walked and they walked,
They walked you to the grave,
Where ends many a one—
Ends many a one.

We watched the mould fall
On your last roof-tree;
Then she went on her way
With a rose in her hair,
And I alone with no other one—
With no other one!

MARY M. COLUM.

Welcome My World

MY WHITE tiger bounding in the west!
  Only eternal, animal and dumb,
   Give me my merited rest.
The end of Time is when my time is come.

My two arc-lamp globes muttering light
My thorax of wild woodbine offered
   Staid, fiery and slight.
My dark room where voiceless chairs are proferred.

My green dragon from the barbarous east!
Bring the light with ropes of shaken rain
   April swells in yeast,
A baffled virgin with a knocking brain;

The flesh bound in flat, rasping scales,
Reptile, to your fugacity I cling.
   My witch of nursery tales,
My everything, my thou, my everything!

Gannets casually stab the sea.
Each hunting wave envies the next its pleasure,
   Surround me
The spine is blank, body is pure measure.

Marble protectress with vigilant breasts,
His enemy armed against the curious sun,
   Safe in the dark, the chests
May be opened and your treasure won.

343

My black tortoise from the hatching north!
Geysers and hissing streams, the landlocked sea
   Are back and forth
Beneath the snail and the sleeper with crooked knee.

My olive naiad in Ionian creeks
My ballad maiden raped in Highland forays,
   World all in fable speaks,
My gun-flanked heroine of detective stories.

Rise and look out the window and dress,
Mother with child, old man with mottled laughter,
   World, be my guest!
And sleep again, go to sleep after

My feast: I'm blind! if oiled athletes preen
Their animal in the glass, if priests refute
   Seen with divine unseen,
I'm dumb, my world, without your light, I'm mute.

Return my early my Lisbon rapture, the galleons
Glittered in from Goa rich and mean,
   Immoderate life stallions,
And the sky in chevalier plume-doff of green

And scarlet kept the burghers in suspense:
Flitter and flit, let others envy me,
   Starling, starlet, what pretense
Could any mortal make to let you be?

Dancing with you is dancing with
Water, ashes kindle on my mouth
   To inform you with,
O my red phoenix from the south!
                              DENIS DEVLIN.

At My Whisper

OH DANAAN brethren,
   undiminished Pagans,
at my whisper passed into your crafty solitudes,
like the discarnate voice of wind that breathes through heady
   mountain grass,
the divulged ecstatic message of desire—
at my whisper gather—

host that Balor slew with his insulting band and pierced through
   his dark eye with instructed shaft,
so by me stand against the leaguering troops of dark and her mine
   made by love restore out of their impious hand.

Lugh, stretch forth your arm,—
   still from the outside of the camp and from the tent door drive
      the opprobrious brood,
oh, yet great brother, consult my heart's embattled wish, my
   soul's desire,
and as from chariot of thy noonward fire, bring me unto my bed
my choice from among women, truly to heal and bless.

Lord Angus, rise anew,
   fort-builder, triumpher, lover, come,
   where Boinn by your red sedge-girt nest at Brugh
   from under spring-green Carberry swells bubbling to renew
   her floods of peace—with the blossom-drops
      of the apple-tree of Emain indue the verdant lawn—
come that I prevail utterly
   that Carberry's wave, with sweet of meadow-floods
   shed on, by Tara and Navan
   endow the fallow plain.

LYLE DONAGHY.

The Deserted Kingdom

"THE King is gone," the old man said,
    As he went utterly alone
Along the ruined walls of stone,
With monkeys chattering overhead,
    "The King is gone. The King is gone,

"I may not question why he chose
    To reign far hence in foreign lands;
    I only wait for his commands,
Contented if he ever knows
    I bow not to the monkey bands.

"So I wait here and watch the gate,
    As I have done through all his reign,
    Lest one day he should come again,
Though all the halls are desolate
    And like enough I watch in vain.

"I fear that if he comes not soon
    The last hinge of the gate I guard
    Will rust across, and wolf and pard
Will prowl in underneath the moon
    And nothing will be left to ward;

"Already broken are the domes,
    Already cracked the outer walls,
    And all the lovely palace falls;
Untended are the princely homes,
    Across whose sills the jungle crawls.

346

"The monkeys look at me and mock;
  They know my King is overseas;
  They deem that he has fled from these!
Whereof they boast from every rock
  And chatter triumph from the trees.

"And yet I guard the gateway well,
  And yet I wait for his commands,
  And hope some traveller of far lands
May one day come to him and tell
  I bow not to the monkey bands."

LORD DUNSANY.

Mary Hynes

(After the Irish of Raftery)

THAT Sunday, on my oath, the rain was a heavy overcoat
 On a poor poet, and when the rain began
In fleeces of water to buckleap like a goat
I was only a walking penance reaching Kiltartan;
And there, so suddenly that my cold spine
Broke out on the arch of my back in a rainbow,
This woman surged out of the day with so much sunlight
I was nailed there like a scarecrow,

But I found my tongue and the breath to balance it
And I said: "If I bow to you with this hump of rain
I'll fall on my collarbone, but look I'll chance it,
And after falling, bow again."
She laughed, ah, she was gracious, and softly she said to me,
"For all your lovely talking I go marketing with an ass,
I'm no hill-queen, alas, or Ireland, that grass widow,
So hurry on, sweet Raftery, or you'll keep me late for Mass!"

The parish priest has blamed me for missing second Mass
And the bell talking on the rope of the steeple,
But the tonsure of the poet is the bright crash
Of love that blinds the irons on his belfry,
Were I making an Aisling I'd tell the tale of her hair,
But now I've grown careful of my listeners
So I pass over one long day and the rainy air
Where we sheltered in whispers.

When we left the dark evening at last outside her door,
She lighted a lamp though a gaming company
Could have sighted each trump by the light of her unshawled poll,
And indeed she welcomed me
With a big quart bottle and I mooned there over glasses
Till she took that bird, the phoenix, from the spit;
And "Raftery," says she, "a feast is no bad dowry,
Sit down now and taste it!"

If I praised Ballylea before it was only for the mountains
Where I broke horses and ran wild,
And not for its seven crooked smoky houses
Where seven crones are tied
All day to the listening top of a half door,
And nothing to be heard or seen
But the drowsy dropping of water
And a gander on the green.

But, Boys! I was blind as a kitten till last Sunday.
This town is earth's very navel!
Seven palaces are thatched there of a Monday,
And O the seven queens whose pale
Proud faces with their seven glimmering sisters,
The Pleiads, light the evening where they stroll,
And one can find the well by their wet footprints,
And make one's soul;

For Mary Hynes, rising, gathers up there
Her ripening body from all the love stories;
And, rinsing herself at morning, shakes her hair
And stirs the old gay books in libraries;
And what shall I do with sweet Boccaccio?
And shall I send Ovid back to school again
With a new headline for his copybook,
And a new pain?

Like a nun she will play you a sweet tune on a spinet,
And from such grasshopper music leap
Like Herod's hussy who fancied a saint's head
For grace after meat;
Yet she'll peg out a line of clothes on a windy morning
And by noonday put them ironed in the chest,
And you'll swear by her white fingers she does nothing
But take her fill of rest.

And I'll wager now that my song is ended,
Loughrea, that old dead city where the weavers
Have pined at the mouldering looms since Helen broke the thread,
Will be piled again with silver fleeces:
O the new coats and big horses! The raving and the ribbons!
And Ballylea in hubbub and uproar!
And may Raftery be dead if he's not there to ruffle it
On his own mare, Shank's mare, that never needs a spur!

But ah, Sweet Light, though your face coins
My heart's very metals, isn't it folly without pardon
For Raftery to sing so that men, east and west, come
Spying on your vegetable garden?

We could be so quiet in your chimney corner—
Yet how could a poet hold you anymore than the sun,
Burning in the big bright hazy heart of harvest,
Could be tied in a henrun?

Bless your poet then and let him go!
He'll never stack a haggard with his breath:
His thatch of words will not keep rain or snow
Out of the house, or keep back death.
But Raftery, rising, curses as he sees you
Stir the fire and wash delph,
That he was bred a poet whose selfish trade it is
To keep no beauty to himself.

PADRAIC FALLON.

The Cool Gold Wines of Paradise

THE God who had such heart for us
   as made Him leave His house,
come down through archipelagos
of stars and live with us
has such a store of joys laid down
their savors will not sour:
the cool, gold wines of Paradise,
the bread of Heaven's flour.

He'll meet the soul which comes in love
and deal it joy on joy—
as once He dealt out star and star
to garrison the sky,
to stand there over rains and snows
and deck the dark of night—
so, God will deal the soul, like stars,
delight upon delight.

Night skies have planet-armies, still
the blue is never full;
rich, massive stars have never bowed
one cloud-bed's flock of wool;
red worlds of dreadful molten fire
have singed no speck of air:—
all is in place, and, each to each,
God's creatures show His care.

The soul will take each joy He deals
as skies take star on star,
be never filled, be never bowed,
be airy, as clouds are,
burn with enlarging heat and shine
with ever-brightening ray,
joyful and gathering thirst for joy
throughout Unending Day.

ROBERT FARREN.

From Disciple to Master

MY LIFE is like a dream,
　I do not know
How it began, nor yet
How it will go.

Out of the night a bird
Has quickly flown
Across the lighted room,
And now is gone

Into the dark again
From whence it came—
So the old druids said,
And I the same.

But we are not content,
I, like them too,
Questioning all I meet,
Seek something new.

Saying to each who comes,
'So much is clear,
But, if you know of more,
I wait to hear.

'The dark, the lighted room,
The bird which flies
Are not enough for man,
Who one day dies.

'Are not enough for man,
That bird which came
Out of the dark and must
Return again.

'If you know more besides,
Tell what you know,
O wise and travelled souls,
Before I go.'

MONK GIBBON.

The Forge

THE forge is dark
The better to show
The birth of the spark
And the Iron's glow.
The forge is dark
That the smith may know
When to strike the blow
On the luminous arc
As he shapes the shoe.

The bellows blows on the dampened slack,
The coal now glows in the heart of the black.
The smith no longer his arm need raise
To the chain of the bellows that makes the blaze.
I see him search where the blue flames are
In the heart of the fire to find the bar,
With winking grooves from elbow to wrist
As he tightens the tongs in his bawdy fist,
As he hands the bar to his fidgety son
Who holds it well on the anvil down
Till he raises the hammer that stands on its head
And he brings it down with a sound like lead,
For fire has muffled the iron's clamour,
While his son beats time with a smaller hammer,
And the anvil rings like a pair of bells
In time to the beat that the spark expels,
And I am delighted such sounds are made,
For these are the technical sounds of trade
Whose glad notes rang in the heavens above
When a blacksmith slept with the Queen of Love.

355

The horse is looking without reproof
For the leathery lap that has hugged his hoof:
The patient horse that has cast a shoe;
The horse is looking; and I look too
Through the open door to the cindered pool
That a streamlet leaves for the wheels to cool.
I meditate in the forge light dim
On the will of God in the moving limb,
And I realize that the lift and fall
Of the sledge depends on the Mover of All.

O lend me your sledge for a minute or two
O smith, I have something profound to do!
I swing it up in the half-lit dark,
And down it comes in a straightening arc
On the anvil now where there's nothing to glow.
What matter? No matter! A blow is a blow!
I swing it up in my bulging fists
To prove that the outside world exists;
That the world exists and is more than naught—
As the pale folk hold—but a form of thought.
You think me mad? But it does me good,
A blow is a measure of hardihood.
I lift the sledge, and I strike again
Bang! for the world inside the brain;
And if there's another of which you have heard
Give me the sledge and I'll strike for a third.

I have frightened the horse, though I meant it not:
(Which proves that he is not a form of thought).
I shall frighten myself if I ramble on
With philosophy where there is room for none.
I was going to say that the blacksmith's blow—
If I were the Master of Those who Know—
Would give me a thesis to demonstrate
That Man may fashion but not create.
He melts the mountains. He turns their lode
Against themselves like a Titan god.

He challenges Time by recording thought,
Time stands; but yet he makes nothing from naught,
He bends Form back to the shapes it wore
Before the dawn of the days of yore;
He bends Form back to the primal state;
He changes all, but he can't create;
And tamper he cannot with the ways of Fate.
Between ourselves it is just as well,
If Man ruled Fate he would make Life hell.

What have I done?
What shall I do?

No wonder Pegasus cast a shoe
When I succumbed to the English curse
Of mixing philosophy up with verse.
I can imagine a poet teaching;
But who can imagine a poet preaching?
Soon I shall hear the blacksmith scoff:
'The ground is sticky, they can't take off!'
When I press with my thighs and begin to urge
The heavenly horse from the earthly forge.

I know right well that a song should be
Airy and light as the leaf of a tree,
Light as a leaf that lies on the wind,
Or a bird that sings as he sits on the linde,
And shakes the spray when he dives for flight
With bright drops sprinkling the morning light;
For song that is lovely is light and aloof,
As the sparks that fly up from the well-shod hoof.

OLIVER ST. JOHN GOGARTY.

Sea Dawn

FROM Wicklow to the throb of dawn
  I walked out to the sea alone
And by the black rocks came upon
A being from a world unknown.

As proud she sat as any queen
On high, and naked as the air:
Her limbs were lustrous, and a sheen
Of sea-gold flowed from her flowing hair.

And as the spreading sea did swell
With the dawn's strange and brimming light,
Her little breasts arose and fell
As if in concord with the sight.

Faint was the sea sound that she made
Of little waves that melt in sand
While with her honey hair she played
And arched the mirror in her hand.

I watched her lift her head and glance,
Then lean away with grace divine.
I stood enraptured till in chance
Within the glass her eyes met mine.

No eyes had ever such a look,
And then I saw her free her eyes.
They dwelt in mine. Mine they took
With wonder and with no surprise.

My heart was molten. I gave up
My heart as she looked deep in me.
The morning as a crystal cup
Held us within the sky and sea.

"I love the soul within you." Thus
I spoke to her. "Sea woman, come.
Come as new morning dawns for us.
This human earth shall be your home."

She answered only with a moan
That I shall hear until I die,
And in that instant she was gone.
Bare was the rock, silent the sky.

FRANCIS HACKETT.

Charles at the Siege

MARSILIUN at Saragossa, Charles at the siege,
    All Spain at heel, her castles broken, all,
Save only Saragossa, every wall
A crumbling monument and every liege
Dead or a Christian; speak, Blancandrin, speak.
Blancandrin speaking, every lord and baron,
Nodding and silent, strokes his bearded cheek;
Clarin of Balaguet, Estamarin,
Malbien from over sea, all nod to hear
Blancandrin speaking for bright, lovely Spain.
Marsiliun is there, he lends his ear
Also to treachery; and Charlemagne
Plays chess at Cordres and sees the summer pass
And counts, perhaps, the days to Michaelmas.
                    GEORGE HETHERINGTON.

The Old Jockey

HIS LAST days linger in that low attic
  That barely lets out the night,
With its gabled window on Knackers' Alley,
Just hoodwinking the light.

He comes and goes by that gabled window
And then on the window pane
He leans, as thin as a bottled shadow—
A look and he's gone again:

Eyeing, maybe, some fine fish-women
In the best shawls of the Coombe,
Or, maybe, the knife-grinder plying his treadle,
A run of sparks from his thumb!

But, O you should see him gazing, gazing,
When solemnly out on the road
The horse-drays pass overladen with grasses,
Each driver lost in his load;

Gazing until they return; and suddenly,
As galloping by they race,
From his pale eyes, like glass breaking,
Light leaps on his face.

F. R. HIGGINS.

While the Summer Trees Were Crying

ALL EVENING, while the summer trees were crying
   Their sudden realization of the spring's sad death,
Somewhere a clock was ticking and we heard it here
In the sun-porch, where we sat so long, buying
Thoughts for a penny from each other.   Near
Enough it was and loud to make us talk beneath our breath.

And a time for quiet talking it was, to be sure, although
The rain would have drowned the sound of our combined voices.
The spring of our youth that night suddenly dried,
And summer filled the veins of our lives like slow
Water into creeks edging.   Like the trees, you cried.
Autumn and winter, you said, had so many disguises

And how could we be always on the watch to plot
A true perspective for each minute's value.   I couldn't reply,
So many of my days toppled into the past, unnoticed.
Silence like sorrow multiplied around you, a lot
Of whose days counted so much.   My heart revolted
That Time for you should be such a treacherous ally

And though, midnight inclining bells over the city
With a shower of sound like tambourines of Spain
Gay in the teeth of the night air, I thought
Of a man who said the truth was in the pity,
Somehow, under the night's punched curtain, I was lost.
I only knew the pity and the pain.
                              VALENTIN IREMONGER.

Be Still As You Are Beautiful

BE STILL as you are beautiful,
    Be silent as the rose;
Through miles of starlit countryside
    Unspoken worship flows
To find you in your loveless room
    From lonely men whom daylight gave
The blessing of your passing face
    Impenetrably grave.

A white owl in the lichened wood
    Is circling silently,
More secret and more silent yet
    Must be your love to me.
Thus, while about my dreaming head
    Your soul in ceaseless vigil goes,
Be still as you are beautiful,
    Be silent as the rose.

PATRICK MACDONOGH.

Dublin Made Me

DUBLIN made me and no little town
   With the country closing in on its streets
The cattle walking proudly on its pavements
The jobbers the gombeenmen and the cheats

Devouring the fair day between them
A public-house to half a hundred men
And the teacher, the solicitor and the bank-clerk
In the hotel bar drinking for ten.

Dublin made me, not the secret poteen still
The raw and hungry hills of the West
The lean road flung over profitless bog
Where only a snipe could nest.

Where the sea takes its tithe of every boat.
Bawneen and curragh have no allegiance of mine,
Nor the cute self-deceiving talkers of the South
Who look to the East for a sign.

The soft and dreary midlands with their calm canals
Wallow between sea and sea, remote from adventure,
And Northward a far and fortified province
Crouches under the lash of arid censure.

I disclaim all fertile meadows, all tilled land
The evil that grows from it and the good,
But the Dublin of old statutes, this arrogant city,
Stirs proudly and secretly in my blood.

DONAGH MACDONAGH.

Pattern of Saint Brendan

THIS is an evening for a hallowed landfall.
   The land breeze slithers down Brandon
Mountain where stone on stone the monkhives
topple and no prayers drone since twelve evangels
voyaged to find the summer islands.
The light withdraws over the maudlin village
and upended curraghs humped like black cattle,
to follow the copper Atlantic shimmer.
O now could twelve exiles
return from voyaging, staring at wonders and charting
infinity, and raise dripping oars to glide
rejoicing, chanting *laudate* with salty lips cracking,
back from the peril of where the sun founders,
to search for lost Ireland round their cold mountain.

This is the evening. The bleat of melodeons
buckleaps fandangos and whips
up the hobnails to belt at the floorboards.
Thirst gravels the gullet; lads with puffed faces
muster a yowl for slopped foamy porter
and grope for the pence in fist-hoarded purses.
Fug blears the wicks; the sergeant is strutting,
tunic neck-open, bellyband bursting;
Annastatia and Nellie slip off to go pairing
as a tip and a wink to the back of the graveyard.
Goat-music, fumes, the stamp of wild heel-bones,
dust whirling high with the din and the fag-smoke,
cries for a fight and calls for the sergeant,
the anger of louts for a gombeenman's farthing,
follow the dayfall, out to the foundered
islands desired from bleak Brandon Mountain.

This is the evening. Brendan, O sailor,
stand off the mainland, backwater and glimmer,
though kirtles be flittered and flesh be seasalted;
watch while this Ireland, a mirage, grows dimmer.
What have you come for? Why cease from faring
through paradise islands and indigo water,
through vinland and bloomland and carribean glory?
Follow your chart with the smoky sea-monsters;
stay with the bright birds where music is pouring
balm for the hurt souls, and Judas repentant
sits for one day on a rock in the ocean.
Turn from the ghostland, O great navigator;
lower the oars for a legend
of journeys; scan tossed
empty horizons from pole to equator
for Ireland, time-foundered, that Ireland has lost.

Francis MacManus.

On Seeing Swift in Laracor

I SAW them walk that lane again
   And watch the midges cloud a pool,
Laughing at something in the brain—
   The Dean and Patrick Brell the fool.

Like Lear he kept his fool with him
   Long into Dublin's afterglow,
Until the wits in him grew dim
   And Patrick sold him for a show.

Here were the days before Night came,
   When Stella and the other—"slut,"
Vanessa, called by him—that flame
   When Laracor was Lilliput!

And here, by walking up and down,
   He made a man called Gulliver,
While bits of lads came out from town
   To have a squint at him and her.

Still, was it Stella that they saw,
   Or else some lassie of their own?
For in his story that's the flaw,
   The secret no one since has known.

Was it some wench among the corn
   Had set him from the other two,
Some tenderness that he had torn,
   Some lovely blossom that he knew?

For when Vanessa died of love,
  And Stella learned to keep her place,
His Dublin soon the story wove
  That steeped them in the Dean's disgrace.

They did not know, 'twas he could tell!
  The reason of his wildest rages,
The story kept by Patrick Brell,
  The thing that put him with the ages.

Now when they mention of the Dean
  Some silence holds them as they talk;
Some things there are unsaid, unseen,
  That drive me to this lonely walk,

To meet the mighty man again,
  And yet no comfort comes to me.
Although sometimes I see him plain,
  That silence holds the Hill of Bree.

For, though I think I'd know her well,
  I've never seen her on his arm,
Laughing with him nor heard her tell
  She had forgiven all that harm.

And yet I'd like to know 'twere true,
  That here at last in Laracor,
Here in the memory of a few,
  There was this rest for him and her.
                BRINSLEY MACNAMARA.

The Strand

WHITE Tintoretto clouds beneath my naked feet,
  This mirror of wet sand imputes a lasting mood
To island truancies; my steps repeat

Someone's who now has left such strands for good
Carrying his boots and paddling like a child,
A square black figure whom the horizon understood—

My father. Who for all his responsibly compiled
Account books of a devout, precise routine
Kept something in him solitary and wild,

So loved the Western sea and no tree's green
Fulfilled him like these contours of Slievemore
Menaun and Croaghaun and the bogs between.

Sixty-odd years behind him and twelve before,
Eyeing the flange of steel in the turning belt of brine
It was sixteen years ago he walked this shore

And the mirror caught his shape which catches mine
But then as now the floor-mop of the foam
Blotted the bright reflections—and no sign

Remains of face or feet when visitors have gone home.
                                    LOUIS MACNEICE.

Aodh Ruadh O'Domhnaill

JUAN de Juni the priest said
Each J becoming H ;

Berruguete, he said,
And the G was aspirate ;

Ximenez, he said then
And aspirated first and last.

But he never said
And—it seemed odd—he
Never had heard
The spirated name
Of the centuries-dead
Bright-haired young man
Whose grave I sought.

All day I passed
In greatly built gloom
From dusty gilt tomb
Marvellously wrought
To tomb
Rubbing
At mouldy inscriptions
With fingers wetted with spit
And asking
Where I might find it
And failing.

Yet when
Unhurried—
   Not as at home
   When heroes, hanged, are buried
   With non-commissioned officers' bored maledictions
   Quickly in the gaol yard—

They brought
His blackening body
Here
To rest
Princes came
Walking
Behind it

And all Valladolid knew
And out to Simancas all knew
Where they buried Red Hugh.

THOMAS McGREEVY.

A Dublin Ballad: 1916

O WRITE it up above your hearth
  And troll it out to sun and moon,
To all true Irishmen on earth
Arrest and death come late or soon.

Some boy-o whistled *ninety-eight*
One Sunday night in College Green,
And such a broth of love and hate
Was stirred ere Monday morn was late
As Dublin town had never seen.

And god-like forces shocked and shook
Through Irish hearts that lively day,
And hope it seemed no ill could brook.
Christ! for that liberty they took
There was the ancient deuce of pay!

The deuce in all his bravery,
His girth and gall grown no whit less,
He swarmed in from the fatal sea
With pomp of huge artillery
And brass and copper haughtiness.

He cracked up all the town with guns
That roared loud psalms to fire and death,
And houses hailed down granite tons
To smash our wounded underneath.

And when at last the golden bell
Of liberty was silenced—then
He learned to shoot extremely well
At unarmed Irish gentlemen!

Ah! where was Michael and gold Moll
And Seumas and my drowsy self?
Why did fate blot us from the scroll?
Why were we left upon the shelf,

Fooling with trifles in the dark
When the light struck us wild and hard?
Sure our hearts were as good a mark
For Tommies up before the lark
At rifle practice in the yard!

Well, the last fire is trodden down,
Our dead are rotting fast in lime,
We all can sneak back into town,
Stravague about as in old time,

And stare at gaps of grey and blue
Where Lower Mount Street used to be,
And where flies hum round muck we knew
As Abbey Street and Eden Quay.

And when the devil made us wise
Each in his own peculiar hell,
With desert hearts and drunken eyes
We're free to sentimentalize
By corners where the martyrs fell.

DERMOT O'BYRNE.

To Tomaus Costello at the Wars

(From the Irish)

HERE'S pretty conduct, Hugh O'Rourke,
 Great son of Brian, blossoming bough,
Noblest son of noble kin—
 What do you say to Costello now?
If you are still the man I loved
 Hurry and aid me while you can.
Do you not see him at my side
 A walking ghost? What ails you, man?
Brian's son, goal of my song,
 If any thought of losing me
Could bring you grief, my love, my life,
 Beseech this man to let me be.
Yet there's such darkness in his ways,
 Though he a thousand oaths repeat
You must not at your peril doubt
 His strong design to have me yet.
And if the river of my shame
 He ford but once, the frontier crossed,
You will not rule that land again;
 Beyond my will my heart is lost.

Fearsome the forms he courts me in;
  Myriad and strange the arts he plies;
Desire, enchantment of the sight,
  Never dons twice the same disguise,
Sometimes I turn and there he stands,
  A stripling with his bashful air,
Swooping upon me like a hawk;
  My heart is wrested from its lair,
Or as if I were a whore he comes,
  A young blood curious of my fame
With sensual magic and dark rhymes
  To woo and mock me in my shame.
Far to the Ulster wars he flies;
  Some town he sacks—I am the town;
With some light love he charms the night—
  Beguiling her, he brings me down.
And many and many a time he comes
  So much like you in voice and shape
He takes me in his arms unguessed—
  My dearest, how can I escape?
But when he comes in his own form,
  With his own voice, I stand transfixed;
My love deserts its wonted place,
  My mind no longer holds it fixed.
Sweetheart, unless you pity me
  And keep my wavering fancy set
And drive that phantom from my side
  I swear that he will have me yet.
I cannot tear myself in two,
  My love, your love within my mind
Pants like a bird caught in a snare—
  My lover, must you be unkind?
If 'tis not wasted time to plead
  Sweet son of Shuretan, let me be;
The women of the world are yours,
  You grieve my husband, courting me.
O sun-mist of the summer day
  You will find I am no easy game
No graceless, lovesick, moony girl,
  I am not dazzled by a name.

Do not believe what neighbours say,
   I am no harlot as you think;
Long since I gave my love away;
   You must not look at me and wink.
Enchantment of desire is vain,
   I see through every mask you don;
You rascal, pity my good name,
   You thief of laughter, get you gone.
You bandit of the world, away!
   I shall not give your lust release;
Smother the frontier posts in flame
   But let my foolish heart have peace.
Bright blossom of the scented wood,
   Yellow Shuretan's hope and pride,
For love, for money or for rank
   I cannot leave my husband's side.
And since I never shall be yours,
   Your father's trade take up anew
And magnify the northern blood—
   The light of poetry are you,
The stirring of the coals of love,
   The voice by which old griefs are healed,
The mast of the rolling sail of war—
   I may be yours, I shall not yield.
And yet and yet, when all is said,
   All my scolding seems untrue,
My mind to each rebuke replies
   If love I must, I must love you.
And now, God bless you and good-bye,
   Our love perfected, let us part;
Ask me no more or jealousy
   Will crucify my husband's heart.
Silence, my darling! Here he comes!
   Away, although my heart should crack!
Make haste! No words! (God help me now!)
   My love—O God!—do not look back!
               FRANK O'CONNOR.

The Tramp's Song

Irish Refrain: Mar dubhairt an fear fad O.

I LEFT the streets of Galway town,
And walked and walked until I stood
By Barna wood,
Where the grumbling stream runs under the road
I saw the fishes jump for flies.
Isn't it better be young than wise?
As the man long ago said.

The moss was spotted with yellow and blue;
I watched the shadows grow long and brown
As the sun went down;
The sky in the west was scarlet red
And the stream was clear and cold.
Isn't it better have luck than gold?
As the man long ago said.

MARY DEVENPORT O'NEILL.

Sketch

IN THE dark pathways of his Gothic mind
  Grim faces, gargoyle-featured, peer and gape,
Heavy with cloistered sin inhibited,
From many a ruined archway, many a dim
Uncharted grass-grown by-way; and the dead,
But seeing, glassy eyes of things that ape
Sad human likeness, bar the path for him
To where, beyond the gibbering host, lies sweet
The untainted forest—fair and sweet and far,
With its green traceries, sheltering many a shy
Soft forest presence, and many a peeping fawn
Lures with faint notes, miraculously drawn
From the uncouth pipes, to where, on a green floor,
Dim forms are dancing, with dream-motived feet,
Under the quiet of the evening star.

SEUMAS O'SULLIVAN.

Life's Circumnavigators

HERE where the taut wave hangs
 Its tented tons, we steer
Through rocking arch of eye
And creaking reach of ear,
Anchored to flying sky,
And chained to changing fear.

O when shall we, all spent,
Row in to some far strand,
And find, to our content,
The original land
From which our boat once went,
Though not the one we planned.

Us on that happy day
This fierce sea will release,
On our rough face of clay,
The final glaze of peace.
Our oars we all will lay
Down, and desire will cease.

W. R. RODGERS.

No Uneasy Refuge

POETRY is no uneasy refuge, stilly centred,
    with terrors sniffing round it and growling behind
or poised for darting. The poet has killed all the tigers
and poisoned in dews of his affliction the quick vipers:
fear and angers were clean put away before he entered.

Leaving his retreat, he is taken up by a fresh wind
and shown a new creation that knows nothing of losses—
unless, here and there, a frail ghost undoes the close mosses
and teaches half sounds to the silence, sways—even tosses
a mist into the moonlight—bringing far defeats to the mind.

There would be nothing to remember but for the dead.
Wheat will spring up in its season; the beasts of destruction
breed and conspire. The poet hears the near voice of sirens,
is beckoned by magic glints to dangerous environs:
who will retrieve him from the monopoly of tyrants—
from those tinsel suppositions and the suave deduction?

He conquers all—enters the cave—first stooping his head.
Poetry is no uneasy refuge, grimly centred—
but the withdrawal into mystery through a low portal,
the shelter under victory's eagle wings, of a mortal
who has done with all his enemies before he entered.

BLANAID SALKELD.

Under Ben Bulben

I

SWEAR by what the sages spoke
    Round the Mareotic Lake
That the Witch of Atlas knew,
Spoke and set the cocks a-crow.

Swear by those horsemen, by those women
Complexion and form prove superhuman,
That pale, long-visaged company
That air in immortality
Completeness of their passions won;
Now they ride in the wintry dawn
Where Ben Bulben sets the scene.

Here's the gist of what they mean.

II

Many times man lives and dies
Between his two eternities,
That of race and that of soul,
And ancient Ireland knew it all.
Whether man die in his bed
Or the rifle knocks him dead,
A brief parting from those dear
Is the worst man has to fear.
Though grave-diggers' toil is long,
Sharp their spades, their muscles strong,
They but thrust their buried men
Back in the human mind again.

III

You that Mitchel's prayer have heard
'Send war in our time, O Lord!'
Know that when all words are said
And a man is fighting mad,
Something drops from eyes long blind,
He completes his partial mind,
For an instant stands at ease,
Laughs aloud, his heart at peace.
Even the wisest man grows tense
With some sort of violence
Before he can accomplish fate,
Know his work or choose his mate.

IV

Poet and sculptor, do the work,
Nor let the modish painter shirk
What his great forefathers did,
Bring the soul of man to God,
Make him fill the cradles right.

Measurement began our might:
Forms a stark Egyptian thought,
Forms that gentler Phidias wrought.
Michael Angelo left a proof
On the Sistine Chapel roof,
Where but half-awakened Adam
Can disturb globe-trotting Madam
Till her bowels are in a heat,
Proof that there's a purpose set
Before the secret working mind:
Profane perfection of mankind.

Quattrocento put in paint
On backgrounds for a God or Saint
Gardens where a soul's at ease;
Where everything that meets the eye,
Flowers and grass and cloudless sky,
Resemble forms that are or seem
When sleepers wake and yet still dream,
And when it's vanished still declare,
With only bed and bedstead there,
That heavens had opened.
                 Gyres run on;
When the greater dream had gone
Calvert and Wilson, Blake and Claude,
Prepared a rest for the people of God,
Palmer's phrase, but after that
Confusion fell upon our thought.

V

Irish poets, learn your trade,
Sing whatever is well made,
Scorn the sort now growing up
All out of shape from toe to top,
Their unremembering hearts and heads
Base-born products of base beds.
Sing the peasantry, and then
Hard-riding country gentlemen,
The holiness of monks, and after
Porter-drinkers' randy laughter;
Sing the lords and ladies gay
That were beaten into clay
Through seven heroic centuries;
Cast your mind on other days
That we in coming days may be
Still the indomitable Irishry.

VI

Under bare Ben Bulben's head
In Drumcliffe Churchyard Yeats is laid:
An ancestor was rector there
Long years ago, a church stands near,
By the road an ancient cross.
No marble, no conventional phrase;
On limestone quarried near the spot
By his command these words are cut.

> *Cast a cold eye*
> *On life, on death.*
> *Horseman, pass by!*

W. B. YEATS.

SLAINTHE!

Slainthe!

I SPEAK with a proud tongue of the people who were
  And the people who are,
The worthy of Ardara, the Rosses and Inishkeel,
My kindred—
The people of the hills and the dark-haired passes
My neighbours on the lift of the brae,
In the lap of the valley.

To them Slainthe!

I speak of the old men,
The wrinkle-rutted,
Who dodder about foot-weary—
For their day is as the day that has been and is no more—
Who warm their feet by the fire,
And recall memories of the times that are gone;
Who kneel in the lamplight and pray
For the peace that has been theirs—
And who beat one dry-veined hand against another
Even in the sun—
For the coldness of death is on them.

I speak of the old women
Who danced to yesterday's fiddle
And dance no longer.
They sit in a quiet place and dream
And see visions
Of what is to come,
Of their issue,
Which has blossomed to manhood and womanhood—

And seeing thus
They are happy
For the day that was leaves no regrets,
And peace is theirs,
And perfection.

I speak of the strong men
Who shoulder their burdens in the hot day,
Who stand in the market place
And bargain in loud voices,
Showing their stock to the world.
Straight the glance of their eyes—
Broad-shouldered,
Supple.
Under their feet the holms blossom,
The harvest yields.
And their path is of prosperity.

I speak of the women,
Strong-hipped, full-bosomed,
Who drive the cattle to graze at dawn,
Who milk the cows at dusk.
Grace in their homes,
And in the crowded ways
Modest and seemly—
Mother of children!

I speak of the children
Of the many townlands,
Blossoms of the Bogland,
Flowers of the Valley,
Who know not yesterday, nor to-morrow,
And are happy,
The pride of those who have begot them.

And thus it is,
Ever and always,
And Ardara, the Rosses and Inishkeel—
Here, as elsewhere,
The Weak, the Strong, and the Blossoming—
And thus my kindred.

To them Slainthe.

PATRICK MacGILL.

NOTES

NOTES

A.E. (George W. Russell)

When in a class in the Art School in Dublin two young men met and found they shared a visionary mood and experience, something was done to initiate a literary movement in Ireland, for these two, though working together in different spheres, brought a fresh trend into Irish poetry. One was George W. Russell, then working in a department store, and the other was William Butler Yeats, the son of a well-known portrait painter. George Russell established a branch of the Theosophical Society in Dublin. When he came to publish his poems in the Society's magazine he wanted to use the pen-name "Aeon," but the printer set it up as "A.E."; thereafter he used those initials. He was born in the north of Ireland in 1867 and died in England in 1935. His volumes of poetry, mainly mystical but sometimes with a political intention, include 'Homeward: Songs by the way,' 'The Earth Breath,' 'Voices of the Stones'; his Collected Poems were published in 1935. But although he held to a mystical vision, "A.E." was always a man of affairs, earning his living as an organizer of groups of farmers for agricultural co-operative societies, and later editing the organ of the Agricultural Co-operative Society, The Irish Homestead. He painted continuously and was able to sell his pictures. When the Irish Free State came into being he was offered, but declined, a seat in the Senate. To help in the creation of a new Ireland he edited The Irish Statesman. A magnificent orator, he lectured extensively in America. Beside his volumes of poetry he wrote prose works which have a philosophical import; the most solid of them is 'The National Being,' which is a consideration of the state as a work of human imagination.

ALLINGHAM, WILLIAM

When William Butler Yeats began to write poems that had in them the sense of locality he turned to the countryside poems of William Allingham for a pattern. The elder poet, who was born in the county neighbouring Yeats's, had sung the countryside, made over old ballads, shaped popular traditions. But

William Allingham was also a learned man and a considerable artist. He was born in 1824 in Ballyshannon, County Donegal, his father being bank manager in that little town. As a professional litterateur he settled in London, where he moved in the Pre-Raphaelite circle and edited Fraser's Magazine. Amongst his works is an anthology of English poetry with the engaging title of 'Nightingale Valley.' He died in London in 1889.

BANIM, JOHN

The brothers Banim produced in collaboration a series of Irish novels and sketches which still retain a high vitality, the "Tales of the O'Hara Family" which deal with life in their southern Irish county at the beginning of the nineteenth century. John Banim was born in Kilkenny in 1798 and died there in 1844. His verse was occasional, arising out of some public emotion.

BOYD, THOMAS

The date of his birth—it was between 1866 and 1870—is not known for certain, and the place was either Donegal or Lougth. While living in London in desperately straitened circumstances (he was employed by some automatic machine company to collect the pennies out of the machines) he wrote some fine poems for Arthur Griffith's journal in Dublin. The Irish Literary Society in London gave him a better-paid and more congenial job as secretary. Unfortunately his morale was broken by this time. Thomas Boyd was a man of great sensibility, considerable accomplishment and a great deal of learning.

BYRNE, WILLIAM A.

He published his poems under the name of William Dara. He was born in the 1880's and died in the 1930's. Living a very secluded life as a teacher in Catholic colleges, little was known about him. From his collection of poems, "A Light on the Broom," one might think he was a lay brother in a monastery.

CALLANAN, JEREMIAH JOSEPH

This poet brought, in one instance, anyway, a recognizable Gaelic cadence into translations from the Irish. That cadence is in "The Outlaw of Loch Lene." Jeremiah Joseph Callanan was born in Cork in 1795. He studied to be a priest, then studied to be a doctor, wandered about Ireland a great deal, and died in Portugal of tuberculosis in 1829.

394

CAMPBELL, JOSEPH

He was born in Belfast in 1879 and published his first collection of poems under the Gaelic form of his name, Seosamh Mac Cathmhaoil. These collections are 'The Mountainy Singer,' 'Irishry,' 'Earth of Cualann.' In his later years his appearance and his delivery of his poems were really bardic. He was a member of the insurrectionary group in 1916, but did not take an active part in the insurrection. After the treaty he was imprisoned by the Free State Government. He then came to America, where he founded a school of Irish Studies. He returned to Ireland and died in his cottage in the Dublin hills in 1944. Many of his poems in their musical settings live among unreading people as folk songs.

CAMPBELL, NANCY

The wife of Joseph Campbell. She has published only a small collection of poems.

CARBERY, ETHNA

This was the pen-name of Anna Johnston. She married Seumas MacManus, the storyteller and poet, but died in the early days of their marriage. Her charming poems, first published in Arthur Griffith's journal, The United Irishman, with their overtones of Gaelicism and strong nationalism, were exciting in the early days of the literary movement. She was born in the north of Ireland, in Ballymena, in 1866 and died in 1902. Her volume of poems, "The Four Winds of Erinn," was published after her death.

Her "Shadowy House of Lugh" needs a note. In Celtic mythology, Lugh is the Sun-god. He is the deliverer of the De Danaans, the Divine Folk, from the Fomorian oppression. He is the slayer of Balor, the glance of whose eye is death. But Lugh is also kin to Balor, his mother being Eithlinn, the daughter whom Balor had immured in a tower.

CARLIN, FRANCIS

This poet's actual name was Francis MacDonald, but he wrote under his mother's name, Carlin, because her family, he thought, had connection with O'Carolans. He spent the greater part of his life in America, working for years as a floor walker in one of New York's department stores. He published his first book of poems, "My Ireland," in New York in 1917. About five years afterwards he disappeared from the circles he was known in and entered a monastery, perhaps as a lay brother. He came back in 1940 and mentioned in an interview that he had written a long religious poem. He died soon afterwards, and nothing is known about the poem he spoke of. He had gone from America to Ireland as a boy and worked on his family's farm in Tyrone and was tremendously influenced by the landscape, people and traditions of that part of Ulster. Out of that experience came the poems in "My Ireland" and his second volume, "A Cairn of Stars." The poem of his given here requires a note. "Redmond O'Hanlon," Francis Carlin wrote "was born about 1623 in the County Armagh where his father owned several townlands. During the Cromwellian settlement this estate was taken over by the English. Then Redmond and his three brothers took to the hills as 'Rapparees.' He went to France where he was given the title of Count, which title was credited to him in the French gazettes. He returned to Ireland before 1671 and became the leader of the 'Rapparees' of Ulster. Having refused to bear witness against the Primate, Oliver Plunkett, one hundred pounds was offered for his head by Ormonde, the Viceroy of Ireland. He was slain in his sleep by a clansman who brought his head to Downpatrick gaol. The Receiver's Book in the Dublin Record Office contains the following entry. 'Paid to Art O'Hanlon as a reward for killing Redmond O'Hanlon, a proclaimed Rebell and Traytor, as by Concordation dated 6th. May 1681—One Hundred Pounds.' " The nearest translation of 'Rapparee' would be 'Guerrilla.' The disbanded Irish armies formed the nucleus for these bands. They levied toll on the planters who had taken over the confiscated estates; they avenged some of the wrongs inflicted on the peasantry, and they checked the exactions of 'The Bashaws of the West and South,' as the historian Lecky calls the new landowners. See also the note on the poet Gavan Duffy.

CASEMENT, ROGER

Roger Casement was born in Dunleary, outside Dublin in 1864. As a young man he entered the British Consular service, and, when he was about forty, was selected for a dangerous mission— the investigation of atrocities committed on the natives of the Belgian Congo. The publication of his report created an immense stir in a Europe that then was unused to atrocity and led to a reform in the administration of the territory. Soon afterwards he was selected for a more dangerous mission, the investigation of atrocities on the natives of the Putumayo on the Amazon. He was knighted by the British government for conduct and reports that reflected such glory on the Consular service, and at the age of forty-eight retired from the service with the idea of devoting the rest of his life to the cause of Irish liberation. The Ireland he returned to was in a revolutionary temper. Casement backed the creation of a volunteer force which might be used to establish and protect a national government. He foresaw a war between England and Germany, and believed that Ireland should put herself on Germany's side. When the war came he went to America to get help from American-Irish groups for the Volunteers. From America he went to Germany which was then at war. Returning to Ireland on a German submarine he was arrested, put on trial in London, and hanged as a traitor in 1916. As against all the charges that would make Casement appear a dishonorable man there stand as witnesses the words of his great report on Putumayo. "It may be long before a demoralization drawing its sanction from so many centuries of indifference and oppression can be uprooted; but Christianity owns schools and missions as well as dreadnoughts and dividends. In bringing to that neglected region and to those terrorized people something of the suavity of life, the gentleness of mind, the equity of intercourse between man and man that Christianity seeks to extend, the former implements of her authority should be more potent than the latter." Roger Casement published a small book of verse which in the main was the rhetoric of politics. The one personal poem is that given in this anthology.

CASEY, JOHN KEEGAN

Was born in 1846 in County Westmeath. As a very young man he belonged to the revolutionary organization of the '60's, the Fenian organization, and was imprisoned for some time. His "Rising of the Moon" keeps the romance and fervour that went with insurrectionary feeling in those days. He died in 1870.

CLARKE, AUSTIN

Was born in 1896. In his early period this poet was fascinated by the saga material and wrote narrative poems out of it— "The Vengeance of Finn," "The Cattle Drive in Connaught"— but has since turned to the theatre and written verse-plays. He is the poet who has most consistently tried to give a Gaelic pattern to the verse he writes in English. He does this by making assonance more important than full rhyme. One of his poems given in this anthology is entitled "Aisling." The Aisling was the distinctive form developed by the Gaelic poets of the seventeenth and eighteenth centuries; the word means 'vision': the poet encounters a beautiful woman who is Ireland, and there is a tragic communion between the two.

COLUM, MARY M.

Born in Ireland, and came to America with her husband, Padraic Colum, in 1914. Author of "From these Roots" and "Life and the Dream." She is best known as a literary critic; has contributed critical articles to most American publications, and was literary critic of Forum Magazine for seven years.

COLUM, PADRAIC

Was born in the midland county of Longford where his father was master of a workhouse at the end of 1881. In his twenties he was associated with Yeats and A.E., and with Arthur Griffith, the founder of the Sinn Fein movement. In Arthur Griffith's journal his poems first appeared. He was a member of the society that founded the national theatre, and wrote plays for the Abbey Theatre—The Land, the Fiddler's House, Thomas Muskerry. He came to America with his wife in 1914. Besides poetry and plays he has written novels and a series of books for children. A note is needed on his versions of "The Islands of the Ever Living"; it is from "The Voyage of Bran" which was translated by Kuno Meyer, the verse portions of which belong to the eighth, or perhaps to the seventh century.

CORKERY, DANIEL

Was born in County Cork in 1878. He lives in his native city, where he is Professor of English Literature in the University. He is a novelist, short story writer and dramatist as well as a poet. As a literary historian he has written a very impressive book on the Gaelic poets of the seventeenth and eighteenth centuries—"The Hidden Ireland." As a critic he stands firmly for the 'Irish-Ireland' idea in literature.

COUSINS, JAMES

Was born in 1873 in Belfast. In his early career he belonged to the society that created the national theatre, and a play of his was produced by them. Subsequently he went to India, where he has remained as a professor of English literature.

CURRAN, JOHN PHILPOT

Was born in County Cork in 1750 and died in Dublin in 1817. He was councillor-at-law in a period when men with such office were the main defenders of individual and national liberty. As an orator he was not surpassed by any of the great speakers of the time, not even by Grattan, and his defence of Peter Finnerty is one of the great pieces of forensic eloquence. He was a member of the Irish Parliament and strove very fervently against its abolition. John Philpot Curran was closer to the people than any other man of his position at the time; he spoke Irish. The poem given in this anthology represents the first attempt—very likely unconscious—to give Gaelic structure to a poem in English: its proper title is "The Deserter's Meditation."

DARLEY, GEORGE

Was born in 1795 in the district which rises to the Dublin hills where his family had long been resident. He was an odd combination—a mathematician as well as a poet. He lived in London the greater part of his life and wrote essays as well as verse. His most distinctive poem is the learned and headlong "Nepenthe," out of which the poem given in this anthology has been extracted. Darley died in London in 1846.

Robert Bridges made this note on "Nepenthe" (not the long poem but the extract). "The Phoenix personifies the earth life of sun-joys, i.e. the joys of the sense. She is sprung of the Sun and is killed by the Sun. It is of the essence of sun-joys to be, in their sphere, as eternal as their cause; and their personification is without ambition to transcend them. The Phoenix is melancholy as well as glad; the sun-joys would not be melancholy if they did not perish in the using: but they are ever created anew. Their inherent melancholy would awaken ambition in the spirit of man. In the last stanza *Mountainless* means 'void of ambition,' and *unechoing* means 'awakening no spiritual echoes.'

DAVIS, THOMAS

Born in County Cork 1814, he died in Dublin 1845. At the age of thirty he had become the hope of the Young Ireland movement, which was the opposition to O'Connell's wordy and legalistic Repeal of the Union movement. Thomas Davis initiated in Ireland that outcome of the Romantic Movement, the realization of the importance of national culture, which had already come to leaders in Bohemia and Finland. With Gavan Duffy he founded the Nation newspaper in which he preached the necessity of recovering the national traditions. Had not circumstances been adverse—the dreadful famine of 1847 came five years after the founding of the Nation—there would have been a cultural movement while Ireland was still largely Gaelic-speaking, with an immense amount of saga, poetry and music in the peoples' possession. The veneration given to this young leader came, one can believe, from a sense on the peoples' part that he had an historic role. His own verse is generally in the form of a ballad with a strong and stirring rhythm, based on an historical episode. In his "Lament for the Death of Eoghan Ruadh O'Neill"—it was the first ballad he published and it initiated a theme and treatment carried on for a long time—the episode is the hearing of the death of the general by one of his clansmen. It was laid to poisoning, but it was not from such an act of treachery: his death was from disease. Eoghan Ruadh O'Neill (Owen Roe) was a nephew of the great O'Neill of Tyrone, the leader in the previous war. He acquired European fame while in the Spanish service and came over to Ireland to serve the Gaelic and Anglo-Irish who had formed the Catholic Confederation. He had the loyalty of the Gaelic but not of the Anglo-Irish party in the war of 1641-49. His victory over the Scottish army at Benburb was the only inspiring action in that dilatory war. He died as Oliver Cromwell unified the English command in Ireland, and perhaps the most unfortunate thing about his death was that it deprived the Confederation of a leader with whom Cromwell could have made a peace. Owen Roe is buried in an island in Lough Oughter in County Cavan.

DERMODY, THOMAS

Was born in Ennis, County Clare, in 1775, and died in London in 1882 in a destitute condition. As a scholar and a verse-writer he was an infant prodigy. After a quarrel with a patron of his in Dublin he enlisted in the British Army, was in some campaigns, and got out of military life with a small pension which he sold. As a boy he showed great promise; he was discovered in rags in a Dublin bookshop, and at the age of twelve excited scholars by his knowledge of Greek and Latin and by verse that he had already written. But he was quarrelsome and drunken, and misfortune pursued him. His most distinctive work is in the satires he wrote when very young.

DE VERE, AUBREY

Was the son of Sir Aubrey de Vere and was born in Adare, County Limerick, in 1814. He was a scholar and held a chair in University College, Dublin, and was a close friend of Cardinal Newman who founded that institution. He died in 1902.

DEVLIN, DENIS

Born in Scotland in 1908. He is in the Irish diplomatic service and has been attached to the Legation in Washington. His *Lough Derg and Other Poems* was published in 1946.

DOWLING, BARTHOLOMEW

Was born in County Kerry in 1823. For some years he was an office holder in Cork and contributed poems to Thomas Davis's Nation. Then he emigrated to America, where the single poem that he is known by was written. He died in San Francisco in 1863.

DUFFY, CHARLES GAVAN

Was born in Monaghan in 1816. With Thomas Davis he founded the Nation in 1842. He was more politically minded than Davis, and he made a statesman-like attempt to bring about an alliance between the Catholic and Protestant farmers of Ireland in 1852. Frustrated in this enterprise he emigrated to

Australia, where his political talents gave him a second career which culminated in a premiership and a knighthood. Leaving Australia in 1880 he attempted to enter Irish affairs once more, but the new political forces were against him. He died where he had been residing for some time, in the South of France, in 1903.

DUNSANY, LORD

Descendant of a famous Norman-Irish family, the eighteenth Baron Dunsany was born in 1878. Besides the poems which have now appeared in "Fifty Poems," he has written brilliant plays, the most notable of which are "The Gods of the Mountain" and "King Argamines and the Unknown Warrior." He is the only modern writer who can be mythological and fabulous.

FALLON, PADRAIC

Was born in Galway in 1906 and grew up amongst a Gaelic-speaking people. The poem of his given in this anthology is not a translation of Raftery's famous poem to Mary Hynes, but is, with its extravagance and its Gaelic fantasy, a dramatization of Raftery himself.

FARREN, ROBERT

Was born in Dublin in 1909. He has been a school teacher and is now a director of broadcasting on Radio Eireann. He put the life of Colum-cille into verse in "This Man was Ireland" and has written a critical work in "The Course of Irish Poetry."

FERGUSON, SAMUEL

Was born in Belfast in 1810 and died in Howth, outside Dublin, in 1886. He was the one elder poet who had a powerful influence on the movement that began with Yeats in the 1880's, for Ferguson had shaped some of the saga material in "Lays of the Western Gael" and "Congal." But his greatest achievement was in his translations of Gaelic folk song: "Cashel of Munster" is one of the three or four poems that carry over a Gaelic rhythm; it has also the wildness of some man dispossessed of everything warm and familiar; the tenderness of the Gaelic folk-song is in his "Dear Dark Head." Samuel Ferguson was an antiquarian and a scholar, and was knighted and made President of the Royal Irish Academy for his research and discoveries.

His translation of "The Fair Hills of Ireland" needs a note. The original was made by Donnchad Ruadh MacNamara, a Munster poet, about 1730. The refrain has nothing to do with hills. The original is sung to the noblest of Irish traditional airs.

FIGGIS, DARRELL

Was born in Dublin in 1882, and, in his twenties, combined business, wandering and adventure for a few years before he launched himself as a writer. His first publication was a volume of poems to which G. K. Chesterton wrote an introduction. This was in 1910. He then wrote a verse play which got a production. At this time he lived in London as a journalist. He had started as a novelist when he came back to live with his wife in Ireland, first in Achill and then in Dublin. He threw himself into the revolutionary movement which then centered round the Volunteers, and it was he who was selected to purchase, secretly, of course, munitions for them on the Continent. This he did successfully and helped to land them at Howth. He was high in the council of Sinn Fein after that and was trusted by Arthur Griffith, who made him chairman of the committee that drew up the constitution for the provisional government. He was not trusted by the men who came into power after the death of Griffith, and, going back to his literary and journalist work, he wrote what may well prove a lasting book, "The Return of the Hero," which he published under the pseudonym, "Michael Ireland." Then disaster came on him. He was writing a book on Blake when his wife shot herself; a young woman he was in love with died miserably; a life which he had vividly imagined for himself, a life in which he would be a statesman and an outstanding literary figure, went out. He committed suicide in London in 1925.

FOX, GEORGE

Is known only for one thing, but that thing is perfect of its kind, the translation from Irish of the "County Mayo." Yeats said of it, "It is as wild as a hare." The original was by Thomas Lavelle or Thomas Flavell, a Connacht poet of the late seventeenth or early eighteenth century.

FOX, MOIREEN

Now Mrs. Chevasse. A strong adherent of Gaelicism, she and her husband lived among the Gaelic-speaking people of Galway and made Gaelic their home language. Her most important work is a narrative poetic sequence, "Liadain and Curitir," which was published in America.

FURLONG, ALICE

Lived in Dublin and was one of the literary group that contributed to Arthur Griffith's United Irishman and Sinn Fein.

FURLONG, THOMAS

Little is known about him except that he was one of the better translators from Gaelic. His poem needs a note. It laments the exile of the native Irish families and the destruction of the Irish woods. The exile and the destruction went together. The woods were destroyed, partly as a measure of safety for the planters—the woods gave shelter to the 'Rapparees'—and partly as a quick way of exploiting the confiscated lands. It was then the deforestation of Ireland began.

GIBBON, MONK

Is related to the Yeats family. He was born in 1906. More than any of the present-day Irish poets he represents the Anglo-Irish tradition that begins with Goldsmith.

GOGARTY, OLIVER

Was born in Dublin in 1878, the son of a well-known doctor. He became a surgeon and a throat specialist. On the establishment of the Irish Free State he was given a place in the Senate and served for fourteen years. Yeats was enthusiastic about his poems. He has written prose also—novels, reminiscences, essays. At present he is living in the United States.

GRAVES, ALFRED PERCIVAL

Was the son of the Protestant Bishop of Limerick and was born in Dublin in 1846. His rollicking song, "Father O'Flynn," made him famous. He lived most of his life in London and was an official of the Board of Education. His son is the well-known poet and prose writer, Robert Graves.

GRIFFIN, GERALD

Was born in Limerick in 1803. With his "Collegians," which was dramatized as "The Colleen Bawn" and turned into an opera as "The Lily of Killarney," he wrote the first, and, for a long time, the most popular Irish novel. But his succeeding novels were dull; he had high hopes for a playwriting career, but in this he was greatly disappointed. Renouncing the literary life he became a Christian Brother; he died in 1840.

GWYNN, STEPHEN

Was born in Donegal in the seventies. He is a poet, scholar, novelist and historian who has written a history of Ireland. For some years he was a Member of Parliament; he has translated several poems from the Middle Irish; the one given in this anthology needs a note.

The Woman of Beare was a courtesan like Villon's Helm-maker, and this dramatization of the courtesan's life belongs to the tenth century.

HACKETT, FRANCIS

Was born in Kilkenny, the son of a doctor who in Parnell's time was active in the political crisis. Francis Hackett came to the United States as a young man and for some years was literary editor of The New Republic. He has written a History of Ireland and several books of literary criticism. He returned to Ireland and lived in Wexford with his wife, Signe Toksvig, for ten years. Subsequently he and she went to live in Denmark, a country which he greatly admires. At present he is living in the United States.

HETHERINGTON, GEORGE

Born in 1916. He has not yet published a collection of his verse. He lives in Dublin where he is connected with a well-known printing establishment.

HULL, ELEANOR

Was born in Dublin in 1860 and died in 1935. She came of a scholarly family, and she herself was an excellent scholar; she wrote the valuable "Text Book of Irish Literature." She made fine translations from the Middle and Modern Irish. Two of her translations given in this anthology need notes.

The original of the beautiful "Sleep Song of Grainne over Dermuid" is given in "Dunaire Finn" (The Poem Book of Finn). Grainne, the affianced wife of Fionn MacCumhal, is fleeing with Dermuid, one of Fionn's paladins. The linnet twitters, the grouse flies, the wild duck pushes out from the stream—everything around signals to Grainne that pursuers are close. The poem is dramatic in its blend of affection and alarm, all set to the soothing measure of a lullaby. In "The Lay of Prince Marvan," the hermit who is brother of Guaire, king of Connacht, praises the hermit's life above the royal state and convinces the king that a hermit's life is better than the prince's that he wants him to return to. Scholars say that this poem belongs to the tenth century. The "Dirge for Art O'Leary," with its improvisations and reminiscences is the typical Irish *caoine*. But the sweep of personal feeling in it puts it apart from all others. Art O'Leary, like many of the Irish gentry of his time, had been abroad; he was an officer in the Hungarian service. He married Eileen of the Raven Hair, the daughter of O'Connell of Derrynane, whose grandson was to be Daniel O'Connell the Liberator. The immediate cause of the tragedy was the winning by O'Leary's mare of a race. At that time Irish Catholics were not permitted to own a horse worth more than ten pounds. The English planter whose horse had been beaten offered O'Leary that sum for it; he was supposed to take the offer. He refused. Thereupon he was declared an outlaw and was afterwards shot down. This was in 1773. The first intimation his wife received of the tragedy was the arrival of the mare without her rider.

HYDE, DOUGLAS

When, as a divinity student, he entered Dublin University (Trinity College), then definitely opposed to Irish culture in any form, Douglas Hyde was asked what languages he knew. "English, German, French, Latin, Greek, Hebrew," he replied, and added "but I dream in Irish." The son of a Protestant rector, he was born in Roscommon in 1860. While in Canada where he taught in a university, he became interested in the Indian tribes and learned something of their language and lore. Returning to Ireland he commenced a work that had momentous consequences in Irish history: he began his great collection of folk poetry and folk stories, publishing in his own striking English translations with the originals of the beautiful folk poetry of Connacht which would have been lost had he not collected it from old men and women. His "Love Songs of Connacht" had an important influence on the poetry in English which was written in the decade that followed its publication, for it gave a pattern and a language to the young poets. He wrote poems in Irish under the name An Craoibhin Aoibhinn, and wrote in English "A Literary History of Ireland." From 1893 to 1915 he was the leader of the history-making Gaelic League. He wrote the first play in Irish that was produced in a regular theatre, taking the principal part. When, in 1938, the new Irish Constitution was adopted, he was made President of Eire, which office he held until 1944.

INGRAM, JOHN KELLS

Is celebrated for one poem, "The Memory of the Dead," which he published in the Nation when he was a student. He was a professor in Dublin University (Trinity College) and came to be rather frightened of the revolutionary implications of his early ballad. He was born in Donegal in 1823 and died in Dublin in 1907.

IREMONGER, VALENTIN

Born in 1918. He has worked in the theatre, lives in Dublin where he has a post in the Office of External Affairs.

JOHNSON, LIONEL

Made his Irish nationalism a kind of religion—he was essentially a religious man—but his family's connection with Ireland

405

was remote; indeed, racially, he was more Welsh than he was Irish. He was the most learned of the literary men of the 'nineties, and was probably the last poet who chose to write in Latin. Born in England in 1867 he practically lived his whole life there, dying in London in 1902 from a fractured skull brought about by a fall.

Yeats wrote of him while he was still living: "He has chosen to live among his books and between two memories—the religious tradition of the Church of Rome and the political tradition of Ireland. From these he gazes on the future, and whether he writes of Sertorius or of Lucretius, or of Parnell or of Ireland's dead or of '98, or of St. Columba or of Leo XIII, it is always with the same cold or scornful ecstasy."

JOYCE, JAMES

The author of "Ulysses" and "Finnegans Wake" published only two small collections of poetry—"Chamber Music" at the beginning of his career, and "Pomes Pennyeach" after the publication of "Ulysses." All his poems are intended for music and nearly all, some beautifully, have been set to music. He was born in Dublin in 1882 and died in Zurich in 1941.

KAVANAGH, PATRICK

Was born in 1905 in County Monaghan, the son of a shoemaker as he has told us in his entertaining autobiography, "The Green Fool." His first collection of poems, "The Great Hunger," was published in America in 1947.

KEARNEY, PETER (Cearnaigh, Peadar)

Fought in the insurrection of 1916 in Thomas MacDonagh's command. The marching song he wrote for the Volunteers has become the Irish national anthem. The ballad in this anthology revives the tradition of the street song; it is sung to a haunting air. He was born in Dublin in 1883 and died in 1942.

KETTLE, THOMAS M.

Was born in 1880 in County Dublin, the son of a gentleman farmer who was one of Parnell's lieutenants. His political affiliations were with the Parnellite Party, headed in his time by John Redmond, and he was elected Member of Parliament under the auspices of that party. At the outbreak of the First World War he joined the British Army and was killed in France in 1916.

KICKHAM, CHARLES JOSEPH

Is celebrated in Ireland for his novel, "Knockagow." He was in the revolutionary movement of the 1840's, the Fenian movement, and was imprisoned for a while. He was born in County Tipperary in 1830 and died in 1882. There is a statue of him in the town of Tipperary. All his work deals with that part of Ireland, the valley of the Suir.

LARMINIE, WILLIAM

A contemporary of the younger Yeats and A.E. He was a scholar and critic with an excellent knowledge of Irish; he collected and translated folk tales of the West of Ireland. Larminie was the first who deliberately tried to bring into Irish verse in English the assonances of Gaelic poetry; he succeeds admirably in this in the poem given in this anthology. It is an epilogue to a long poem entitled "Fand," based on the story of the love of Fand, the Sea God's wife, for Cuchullain, and the jealousy of Cuchullain's wife, Emer. A good deal of Larminie's work remains unpublished, notably his translation from the Latin of some of the work of an Irish philosopher of the ninth century, Johannes Scotus Erigina. He was born in County Mayo in 1850 and died in 1900.

LAWLESS, EMILY

The daughter of Lord Cloncurry, she was born in County Kildare in 1845 and died in England in 1913. Besides the poems which she published in a volume entitled "With the Wild Geese" she wrote "With Essex in Ireland" and two novels of the west of Ireland, "Hurrish" and "Grania."

In reading her poem "Fontenoy" it should be remembered that the Irish regarded the battle of Fontenoy (1745) as a national victory. The charge of the Irish Brigade in the French service flung the English back as they were on the point of putting the French to rout. The Irish went into battle with the cry "Remember Limerick"—it signified to them a broken treaty.

LEDWIDGE, FRANCIS

Was born in County Meath in 1891. His early poems attracted the attention of Lord Dunsany, who devoted himself to making the young poet known. He joined the British Army on the outbreak of the First World War and served in Greece for a while. He was in Ireland when his friends, Pearse, MacDonagh and Plunkett, were executed, and was greatly shaken by the event: it was with their fate in mind that he wrote "Lament for the Poets." Returning to the trenches he was killed in Flanders in 1917.

LESLIE, SHANE

Now Sir Shane Leslie. He was born in 1885 on his family's estate in County Monaghan, his mother being one of the Jeromes of New York. Besides his poetry he has written a great many prose volumes.

LETTS, WINIFRED

She was born in 1882, and most of her life has been lived in Dublin. Her most important book is "Songs from Leinster."

LONGFORD

The sixth Earl of Longford was born in 1902 in County Westmeath, and he is a nephew of Lord Dunsany. He has written several remarkable plays and manages the Gate Theatre in Dublin. He has published three volumes of translations of the Irish bardic poems.

MACDONAGH, DONAGH

The son of Thomas MacDonagh, he was born in Dublin in 1912. His volume of poems, "The Hungry Grass," was published in 1947, and his verse comedy, "Happy as Larry," was produced in London the same year.

MACDONAGH, THOMAS

As one of the leaders of the insurrection of 1916 he was executed after the surrender. He was born in Tipperary in 1878. He taught in Padraic Pearse's school and was afterwards a lecturer in the National University. An Irish scholar, he made some very distinctive translations and wrote an important book of criticism, "Literature in Ireland."

MACDONOGH, PATRICK

Was born in 1902. He has published three books of verse, "A Leaf in the Wind," "The Vestal Fire," "Over the Water."

MACMANUS, FRANCIS

Was born in 1909, and is a novelist and critic as well as a poet. He is now a teacher.

His "Pattern of St. Brendan" needs a note. Brendan was the navigator, the story of whose voyages made such a sensation in the mediaeval world and justified the later dreams of sailing into the West. His 'pattern,' a pilgrimage to his birthplace with religious and secular observances, is kept in our time. The poet contrasts the places Brendan sailed to with the place he might be expected to return to, and so makes a bitter satire.

MACMANUS, SEUMAS

Was born in Donegal in 1870. He is a famous teller of stories and has been able to get the traditional form and the traditional lilt of the words on the printed pages. He has published many volumes of stories and a very characteristic biography, "The Rocky Road to Dublin." He lives part of the year in America and part in Ireland, and in his native Donegal.

MacNamara, Brinsley

Was born in County Clare in 1890, and began his career as an actor in the Abbey Theatre. One of his novels, "The Valley of the Squinting Windows," made much disturbance. His plays, novels and poems have the background of County Meath.

MacNeice, Louis

The son of the Protestant Bishop of Down and Connor, he was born in Belfast in 1907. He has lectured on Greek literature, and besides his volumes of poetry he has written plays and criticism dealing with modern poetic trends, including an illuminating book on the poetry of Yeats.

MacNeill, Eoin

As an Irish scholar, Eoin MacNeill's work paralleled Douglas Hyde's. He was vice-president of the Gaelic League while Hyde was president; he dealt with texts while Hyde dealt mainly with the folk traditions; he wrote of ancient Irish laws and institutions while Hyde wrote literary history. Eoin MacNeill was chief of staff of the Volunteers at the time of the insurrection, but did not take part in it. He was imprisoned with the surviving leaders of the Volunteers. Later he had a chair of Irish in the National University. He was born in County Antrim in the seventies and died in Dublin in 1945.

The poem translated, "Aimirgin's Invocation," is traditionally the earliest Irish poem, being supposed to be spoken by Aimirgin, the son of Mile, from the deck of one of the invading ships; it is to bespell as much as to invoke; it is an incantation. The metre of the original is called 'Rosg'; poems in this metre according to Dr. Hyde depended for their effect on rapidity of utterance partly, and partly upon alliteration. In this particular utterance a remarkable effect is gained by the repetition of images as a sort of internal rhyme.

Mahony, Francis

Was born in Cork 1804 and died in Paris in 1866. He was educated in France and Italy, was ordained priest and entered the Jesuit order. Not many duties were exacted from him, and he lived the unattached life of an eighteenth century Abbé in London, Rome and Paris. His active life was given to journalism and social intercourse; he was very learned and very witty, and fond of making erudite jokes. In his writings he called himself "Father Prout," and it was under that name that his one memorable piece, "The Bells of Shandon," appeared. He is buried in Cork close to the Shandon bell turret.

MANGAN, JAMES CLARENCE

Was born in Dublin in 1803 and died in hospital of cholera, a disease rife in Ireland after the famine, in 1849. All his life he was faced by destitution, and in his later days he succumbed to alcohol and opium. John Mitchell has left a picture of him as he saw him in the library of Trinity College on the top of a ladder: the blanched hair was totally unkempt; the corpse-like features still as marble; a large book was in his arms, and all his soul was in the book. In his distinctive poems, "Siberia," "The Ode to Maguire," "The Lament for the Princes of Tyrone and Tyrconnell," he has an unequalled power of evoking a desolate scene, desolate, but in the Irish evocations, with power to inspire undying devotion. He is not always desolate: his "Dark Rosaleen" has exaltation and prophetic fervour; his "Kathleen ni Houlahan" and "Farewell to Patrick Sarsfield" have a sort of gladness about them that comes from worship, in the case of "Patrick Sarsfield," hero-worship.

The Ode to the Maguire was made by the poet of the Maguire family, O'Hussey, who happened to be the most distinguished poet of his time. Hugh Maguire, Prince of Fermanagh, was with Hugh O'Neill and Hugh O'Donnell in the war that came at the end of Elizabeth's reign. "When it is remembered," writes Dr. Hyde, "that O'Hussey composed this poem in the most difficult and artificial of metres . . . it will be seen how much Mangan gained by his free and untrammelled metre, and what technical difficulties fettered O'Hussey's art and lent glory to his triumph over them." Here it should be said that Mangan did not translate directly from the Irish but worked from the prose translations furnished him by the scholar, John O'Donovan.

"The Lament for the Princes of Tyrone and Tyrconnell" comes out of the most tragic happening in Irish history. Hugh O'Neill (the Earl of Tyrone in English history) had been the leader in the last war of a purely Gaelic Ireland against the English in Ireland. He was forced to leave Ireland in 1607; his flight meant the passing of the leadership of the Gaelic nobles and the close of an epoch in Irish history. With O'Neill went the chief representatives of the great Ulster families. The poem is addressed to the Lady Nuala O'Donnell by the bard of the O'Donnells, Mac an Bhaird or Ward. The bard is supposed to discover the Lady Nuala weeping alone over the tomb of her brother, Rory, in the Church of S. Pietro Montorio on the Janiculum. He imagines the whole scene transferred to Ireland

410

(which accounts for the image of horses' hooves rampling down "the mount whereon the martyr-saint was crucified") and he tells her how all Ireland, and especially all Northern Ireland, would join in her grief. Never was the attachment of the Irish to their nobles revealed more poignantly than in this poem which laments the passing of the greatest and truest of the Irish families.

"Dark Rosaleen" and "Kathleen-ni-Houlahan": The original of "Dark Rosaleen" is supposed to be Hugh O'Donnell's address to Ireland at a time when the Irish were expecting help from Spain and from the Pope. This poem probably begins the Irish convention of identifying Ireland with a woman for whom the poet has a mystical devotion. "Dark Rosaleen" is in the aristocratic convention, whereas "Kathleen-ni-Houlahan" (Kathleen, the daughter of Houlahan) is in the peasant convention: this poem was made at a time when the Irish were expecting a restoration of the Stuarts who, they expected, would grant them more liberty than they had under the Puritans.

"A Farewell to Patrick Sarsfield": Sarsfield was the leader of the Irish in the wars that closed the seventeenth century. He is famous in Irish story as the defender of Limerick; his surrender of Limerick meant the end of organized Irish resistance. Then followed the period of the 'Rapparees' or guerrillas. After the surrender Sarsfield with most of his army sailed for France, where they took service with Louis XIV. He was killed at the battle of Landen in 1693. By the way, the name Patrick, or Padraic, came into fashion among the Irish, not out of veneration for the saint, but in memory of Patrick Sarsfield.

McGreevy, Thomas

Born in Kerry in 1893. He served with the British army in the First World War. His main interest is the fine arts on which he has written and lectured a great deal. The poem of his given in this anthology needs a note.

Aodh Ruadh o Domhnaill (Red Hugh O'Donnell), Prince of Tyrconnell, was associated with O'Neill in the last war waged by the Gaelic princes. After the defeat at Kinsale in 1601, he went to Spain to get further help from Philip III, and was there poisoned by an English agent. He was buried in a church that was destroyed in the nineteenth century, the church of San Francisco at Valladolid. The visitor searching for his tomb is told by the guide that certain Spanish names are aspirated, and recalls that in Irish O'Donnell's name has to be aspirated. For his contemporaries, Hugh O'Donnell was always youthful, bright-haired (hence the 'Ruadh' in his name) and impetuous.

411

MEYER, KUNO

Was born in Germany in 1859 and died in Germany—out of which he had been nearly all his lifetime after the First World War—in 1919. A great philologist, he was devoted to Irish literature, and he made some beautiful translations of early Irish poems. His translation of "St. Patrick's Breastplate" needs a note. Like "Aimirgin's Invocation" the original is in the 'Rosg,' and like that poem, too, it is a magical incantation, although the Christian divinity is called upon. It is known to have been current in the seventh century, and it was then ascribed to St. Patrick. It is called the 'Lorica' and also the 'Deer's Cry.' St. Patrick had returned to Ireland where he had been a slave; he was on his way with companions to the High King's seat at Tara where he was to confront the pagan power when he uttered it. Assassins were in wait for him and his companions, but as he chanted the hymn or incantation it seemed to the hidden band that a herd of deer went by.

MILLIGAN, ALICE

Was born in County Tyrone in 1866. Although of a Presbyterian and Unionist family she became a fervent nationalist in her girlhood and with Anna Johnston (Ethna Carbery) founded and edited a nationalist weekly, The Shan Van Vocht, that was a precursor of Gaelic League and Sinn Fein publications. She had plays produced in the early days of the theatre movement. Her single volume of poems, "Hero Lays," reveals, in a sort of practicality that goes with her vision and dream, something northern and womanly.

MITCHELL, SUSAN

Was born in County Sligo. She was associated with A.E. in the editorship of the Irish Statesman. Besides the serious poems published in "The Living Chalice" she wrote witty and satirical verses about the celebrities of the day—"Aids to Immortality of Certain Persons in Ireland." She died in 1930.

MOORE, THOMAS

Was born in Dublin in 1779 and died in England in 1852. He was the first poet of a national awakening—one has to regret, of course, that the first poet had not more range and intensity; he fell heir to the music of his country and to the interest in the Celtic past that MacPherson had awakened. As much a musician as a poet, he wrote verses for the ancient airs that had in his time been recovered from the last of the harpers, verses that were thought to be fitting not only for the music but for

412

the whole tradition out of which the music came. Purely as a song writer, no one has surpassed Thomas Moore. Many times he transcended the limits of song writing and reached poetry: "The Harp that Once through Tara's Halls" is not only magnificent as a song, but it brings us something that is very rare in song or even in poetry, the dignity of a nation's utterance; "At the Mid-hour of Night" with its distinctive rhythm (the rhythm is a Gaelic one) is a memorable lyric, and there are other lyrics of his that are fine in feeling and craftsmanship. Moore's fame and influence should have been eclipsed in the generation that followed his by a poet who would be more assuredly Irish, who would bring into the new national expression the intensity of Gaelic feeling. But the dire conditions of the country prevented the emergence of such a poet from the only group that could have given him the proper endowment, the disinherited Catholic peasantry, and so Thomas Moore remained the representative Irish poet for a prolonged period.

O'BOLGER, T. D.

Was an Irish-born professor in the University of Pennsylvania. The poem given in this anthology appeared in Poetry, Chicago.

O'BRIEN, FLANN

Is a novelist and dramatist as well as a poet, and writes a witty column in a Dublin newspaper under the name "Myles na gCopaleen." No one can get better than he into translation the gracefulness of academic Irish poetry.

O'CONNOR, FRANK

Was born in Cork, 1903, and his baptismal name is Michael Donovan. As a youth he was in the insurrectionary forces, and he has written a volume of short stories, "Guests of the Nation," which deal with incidents of the guerrilla war. He is a fine scholar in Irish, and can bring over, not only the import of the old poems, but their vigour of utterance. The Tomaus Costello of the poem given here was a well-known poet of the seventeenth century. In the poem he is opposed, not only as a lover to a husband, not only as a poet to a soldier, but as a person who, according to the Irish conception of the poet, has a sort of magical force about him. The poem is extraordinary in the fact that it breaks with the impersonal convention that the Gaelic poets worked in; no man could have broken through the convention as the woman-poet in this case has done.

O'CAROLAN, TURLOUGH

Was born in County Meath in 1670 and died in 1738, and so was a contemporary of Jonathan Swift, who took notice of him.

He was a harper and composer rather than a poet, and his poems are occasional, made for some entertainment or in praise of the household of some patron. The poem given in this anthology is addressed to Kian O'Hara of Sligo, one of the two or three Irish princes who had managed to hold on to their estates—in the case of the O'Haras by becoming Protestant.

O'CURRY, EUGENE or EOGHAN

Was born in County Clare in 1796 and died in Dublin in 1862. He and his contemporary, John O'Donovan, were the giants of Irish scholarship. They did what no other scholars since could have done because they inherited the traditional scholarship in language and history. His great work is his "Lectures on the Manuscript Materials of Ancient Irish History."

O'NEILL, MARY DEVENPORT

Was born in Galway, and is the wife of Joseph O'Neill, the author of "Land Under England" and "Chosen by the Queen." Her volume "Prometheus and Other Poems" was published in London in 1937.

O'SULLIVAN, SEUMAS

Was born in Dublin in 1879. His mother's family belonged to the O'Sullivan clan, and so he adopted the name, his family name being James Starkey. He was one of the younger poets associated with Yeats, A. E. and George Moore, and his first book, "The Twilight People," brought a new rhythm into Irish verse. His collected poems were published in America with the title "Dublin Poems." He founded and edits The Dublin Magazine.

PARNELL, FANNY

Was the sister of 'The Uncrowned King of Ireland.' She was born on the family estate in County Wicklow in 1854 and died in the United States in 1882.

PEARSE, PADRAIC

Was born of English and Irish parents in Dublin in 1879 and was executed after the insurrection of 1916. He was named President of the Irish Republic. He had a very full career as editor, educationalist and pamphleteer as well as poet and story-writer. As a poet he wrote in Irish and English, and his poems were translated by his colleague, Thomas MacDonagh.

PETRIE, GEORGE

Was born in Dublin in 1790 and died in 1866. Through his efforts, a great many of the ancient Irish airs were collected just as they were about to disappear, among them the famous

"Londonderry Air." He was a scholar and antiquarian through whose activities a part of the national heritage was saved.

PLUNKETT, JOSEPH MARY

The son of Count Plunkett, was born in Dublin in 1887. He was one of the leaders of the insurrection of 1916 and was executed after the surrender with his colleagues Pearse and MacDonagh. The collection of poems published in his lifetime is entitled "The Circle and the Sword."

RAFTERY, ANTHONY

Was poor, blind and a wanderer, and earned his living by playing the fiddle at wakes and weddings. Once when he was fiddling in a cottage he heard someone ask, "Who is the old fellow over there?" and turning round he made the perfect utterance given in this anthology. His famous poem is to Mary Hynes which is recreated in Padraic Fallon's version. He was born in County Galway in 1784 and died in 1835. His poems have been collected, edited and translated by Dr. Douglas Hyde.

ROLLESTON, THOMAS WILLIAM

Was born in Leix County in 1857 and died in London in 1920. He was able to translate Whitman's "Leaves of Grass" into German. As a translator from the Irish he was amongst the very best, and his "Clonmacnoise" makes a beautiful poem in English. On this and two of his original poems a note is needed.

The monastery and school of Clonmacnoise was founded by St. Kiernan about 544. It grew to be the greatest of the Irish schools. "Some of the most distinguished scholars of Ireland, if not of Europe, were educated at Clonmacnoise," Dr. Hyde says. Clonmacnoise contains two famous sculptured crosses of about 1000 A.D. It was sacked at different times during the invasions. "The Grave of Rury" is about the last High King of Ireland, the Roderick O'Connor of histories written in English. The Treaty of Windsor which he signed stipulated that the office of High King be abolished. The author's note on the poem is as follows: "Ruraidh O'Conchobhar, last king of Ireland, died and was buried in the monastery of St. Fechin at Cong, where his grave is still shown in that most beautiful and pathetic of Irish ruins. All accounts agree in this, but some have it that his remains were afterwards transferred to Clonmacnoise by the Shannon." The title of the other poem of Rolleston's given, "Cois na Tineadh," means "By the Fire."

SALKELD, BLANAID

Has published three volumes of poems, the latest being "The Engine is Left Running," 1937.

SIGERSON, GEORGE

Was born in County Tyrone in 1836 and died in Dublin in 1925. In his student days in Paris he was a pupil of Charcot with Sigmund Freud. He was a neurologist and biologist as well as a literary man and, owing to his Norse descent, was interested in the Norse kingdom of Dublin. In his "Bards of the Gael and Gall" he included translations of poems on Irish subjects written in Norse as well as translations from the Irish. His translation of Cuchullain's Lament over the friend he had slain, Fardiad, sums up all the chivalry and brilliancy of the Irish epic tale, The Tain Bo Cuiligne.

STANIHURST, RICHARD

Represented the old English Catholic stock in Ireland. His father was speaker of the Irish House of Commons in 1557, 1560, and 1568. He was educated in Ireland, at a famous school founded by the Ormond family in Kilkenny, a school that was to have such pupils as Swift and Berkeley. He wrote a "Description of Ireland" and a "Continuation of the Chronicles of Ireland" which were included in Holinshed's "Chronicles." He lamented that in his time the old English district in Ireland, the Pale, was becoming Irish-speaking. As to his metrical work, he insisted that quantity rather than accent should be the guiding principle of English as it is of Latin verse, and, acting on this principle he translated seven books of the Aeneid, using the hexametre. He dedicated his metrical works to the Lord Dunsany of the time who was his brother-in-law. He died in Brussels in 1618.

STEPHENS, JAMES

Born in Dublin 1881. His poems were first published in Arthur Griffith's journal, Sinn Fein, and these, collected, made his first volume, "Insurrections." He published his first narrative, "The Charwoman's Daughter," in the Irish Review, of which he was one of the editors, and this attracted the notice of an American publisher and launched him as a writer with a real public. He then wrote his famous "Crock of Gold" and followed it with his beautiful and humorous narratives based on the old sagas, "In the Land of Youth" and "Deirdre," and his extraordinary "Irish Fairy Tales." His Collected Poems were published in 1926.

SWIFT, JONATHAN

If Stanihurst is claimed as the last of the old Anglo-Irish, Jonathan Swift may be claimed as the first of the new Anglo-Irish writers. He was born in Dublin in 1667, the son, as recent research seems to show, of Sir William Temple's father. Although his ancestry was purely English, he left, by his great pamphlets and his propagandist ballads, a mark on subsequent Irish writing. He was educated in Kilkenny and in Dublin University; was Dean of St. Patrick's, and left his money to an asylum in Dublin. He died in 1745.

SYNGE, JOHN MILLINGTON

Born outside Dublin in 1871 and died in Dublin in 1909. After graduating from Dublin University he went on the continent to study music; he was a good violinist. He lived in Paris for a while on a very small income and then came back to Ireland where he lived in out-of-the-way places, learning Irish and the peoples' dialects in English. These sojourns gave him the rich and vivid speech that he used in his plays. He wrote few poems, but they all have great power. "It may almost be said that before verse can become human again it must learn to be brutal," he wrote in his preface to his "Poems and Translations."

TODHUNTER, JOHN

Was born in Dublin in 1839 and died in London in 1916. He practiced medicine, wrote a play for the Independent Theatre in London, and translated Faust.

TYNAN, KATHERINE (Hinkson)

Born in County Dublin 1861, and died in London 1931. Her volumes of reminiscences of life in Ireland and England in the '90's and 1900's are of great interest. Her Collected Poems were published in 1930.

WALSH, EDWARD

Was one of the early translators of Irish folk poetry. He was born in Derry in 1805 and died in Cork in 1850. He had a strange life for a poet, being schoolmaster to the convicts on Spike Island and afterwards to the paupers in Cork workhouse.

WHITE, JOSEPH BLANCO

Belonged to an Irish family that had emigrated to Spain—hence the 'Blanco' in his name. He was born in Seville, but came to live in England. He regarded himself as an Irishman.

WILDE, OSCAR FINGAL O'FLAHERTIE

Was the son of the distinguished doctor, archeologist and statistician, Sir William Wilde; his mother was a poet who wrote for the Nation under the name of "Speranza." There is no need for a note on his work here. He was born in Dublin in 1854 and died in Paris in 1900.

WOLFE, CHARLES

Like Blanco White Wolfe was a one poem poet; however, he wrote a good deal of verse about Ireland which is no longer remembered. He was born in Dublin in 1791 and died in County Cork in 1823. His "Burial of Sir John Moore," splendid in its masculine feeling, its sense of suspended action and ill-lighted interval, was published anonymously.

YEATS, WILLIAM BUTLER

The greatest of Irish poets was born in Dublin in 1865 and died in France in 1939. He was fortunate in having 'the best father in literary history,' John Butler Yeats, the portrait painter and noted conversationalist. In his early career he took up the tradition in Irish poetry that had been initiated by Allingham and Ferguson, the tradition of local poetry and poetry that was drawn from the old sagas. All his life he was active in the Nationalist movement. Through his efforts and productions a national theatre was created; he became the first dramatist in centuries who was able to hold an audience with his verse plays. On the establishment of the Irish Free State he was made Senator and took an active part in legislation. He left a tradition that is of inestimable value to succeeding Irish poets.

NOTES ON THE ANONYMOUS SONGS AND BALLADS

Allulu mo Wauleen: The title might be translated, "Hail, my little bag." 'Sauleen' means the 'little heel' or end of the bag; 'mo chardas,' 'my dear friend'; a 'dark man' is a blind man. I do not know if this ballad, which was given me by the scholarly Father Power of Waterford, has a Gaelic original, but the number of Gaelic words in it suggests that it is a translation.

The Boyne Water: This is the oldest and most spirited version of the famous Orange song that celebrates the victory of the Williamites over the Jacobites at the battle of the Boyne.

My Love Is Like the Sun: Burns re-wrote some stanzas of this song, and so it sometimes appears in his works. The reference, however, to the Curragh of Kildare stamps it as an Irish popular song.

The Shan Van Vocht: The title is literally "The Poor Old Woman." This was the 'secret' name for Ireland, like 'Roisin

Dubh,' the Little Dark Rose, and "Kathleen-ni-Houlahan," Kathleen the daughter of Houlahan.

The Night before Larry Was Stretched: The poem was written in the Dublin slang of the eighteenth century by some anonymous Villon. At the time there were many ballads celebrating life in gaols and the business of an execution. The coffin was usually sent into the condemned cell "that the sight might suggest the immediate prospect of death and excite corresponding feelings of solemn reflection and preparation for the awful event." The friends of the condemned man were allowed to be with him before the execution, and the coffin was generally used as a card table. There is another ballad comparable to this in its harsh zest of life—the street song, "Johnny, I Hardly Knew You." But, more than the other, "The Night before Larry Was Stretched" shows a most accomplished artist: the unrhymed line at the end of the stanza is extraordinarily effective.

The Oul' Grey Mare: The Napoleonic cause was symbolized by the illiterate ballad makers under various unexpected forms. In this street song made up after Napoleon's downfall the symbol is the old mare that still may have enough calibre to come back and lead the field. The opening stanza, completely in the spirit of the rest of the street song, is a restoration by Padraic Pearse.

INDEXES

INDEX OF AUTHORS

424

INDEX OF FIRST LINES